Vietnam War Memorials

*Dedicated to all those who felt
the pain of the Vietnam War.*

May this help to heal the wounds.

Vietnam War Memorials

*An Illustrated Reference
to Veterans Tributes
Throughout the United States*

by
Jerry L. Strait
and
Sandra S. Strait

McFarland & Company, Inc., Publishers
Jefferson, North Carolina, and London

The authors extend their gratitude to the following sources who granted permission to use their photographs: William L. Nolin, Sr. (pp. 3–4); Leo Bullington (p. 6); Bill Laurie (pp. 8–9); Michael Montgomery (p. 13); Jewell E. Appleton (pp. 19, top, and 26, bottom); Manuel W. Chick Cicogni (p. 19, bottom); Jacques Gael Cressaty, San Francisco (p. 21); California Vietnam Veterans Memorial Commission (p. 24, bottom); M. Edith Penn (p. 26, top); Elvin Porter and the City of Whittier, California (p. 28); Ken Delfino (pp. 29 and 200); Tim Drago (p. 30); William J. McNamara (p. 33, top); James F. Kissane, Jr. (p. 33, bottom); Francis J. Schneider, Jr. (p. 36); John Mastro (pp. 37, 38, 41, 43); Daniel Hohn (pp. 40, 130); Roger M. Brodin (pp. 44, 126); U.S. Dept. of Defense (pp. 46, 47); John Allen (pp. 49, 50); E.J. Flowers (pp. 51, 52); Richard M. Daniels (pp. 58, 67); Jesse A. Lane (p. 62); Robert A. Lynn (pp. 63, 66); Tony George (p. 65); John Snyder (p. 69); Preston Charles (p. 71); American Battle Monuments Commission (p. 72); Julio Gonzalez (pp. 78, 149, top); Till Giron (p. 79); Mike Colin (p. 80); James Lee Highla (p. 82); Michael Ferguson (p. 84); Ronald Sauers, Jr. (p. 86); Gregory P. Gordon (p. 89); Donna F. Wagner (p. 92); Calvin E. Green, Jr. (p. 93, top); C.S.M. Lloyd H. Krohn (Ret.) (p. 93, bottom); Raymond H. Blackman (p. 95); John Francis (p. 97); Larry L. Flink (p. 98, bottom); Michael Waldron (p. 99); Donald W. Buchanon (p. 104); William F. Ryan (p. 105); Loyde P. Arender (p. 106); James F. Ledger (p. 109); Opal E. Clark (p. 110); Roland T. Castronova (pp. 113, 114; p. 116, bottom; p. 117); John T. Likely (p. 116, top); Allen Arlington (pp. 120–123); Douglas D. Lorenz (p. 129); J.P. Stokes (p. 131); Leah Swanger (p. 132); Patrick J. McDermott (p. 136); Gloria Le Droit (p. 137, top); Nebraska City (NE) *News-Press* (p. 137, bottom); Lynn M. Smith (p. 141); Charles J. Zimmerman (p. 145); Edmund A. Davis (p. 149, bottom); 1987 Abbe Godwin, Sculptor, and NC Vietnam Veterans Memorial Committee, Inc.—1987 Stephen A. Acai, Jr., Photographer (p. 152); Leroy M. Fout (p. 158); Beaverton (OR) Elks Lodge #1989 (p. 162); Beaver County (PA) *Times* (p. 165 and p. 166, top); Frances E. Hess (p. 166, bottom, and p. 167); Leonard J. Oniskey (p. 168); Vincent A. Petroff (p. 170, top); Johnstown (PA) *Tribune-Democrat* (p. 170, bottom); Jim Smartz (p. 171); Gary L. Rogers (pp. 177–178); Leo Deurmier (pp. 179–180); Gordon R. West (p. 181); Marvin Bolinger (p. 183, top); June Ownby (p. 183, bottom); Bob Parkins (p. 184); Fred Tucker (p. 185); Butch Rhea (p. 186); Magdalena E. Barnes (p. 189, bottom, and p. 190); Charles Steger (p. 191); Luis Charles, Jr. (p. 193); Rodney Cobb (p. 194); H. Benson Dendy III (pp. 199, 201); Michael Keller (p. 208); Wayne E. Richmond (p. 210, top); Bob Zientara and the Hudson (WI) *Star-Observer* (p. 210, bottom); Dale E. Reich (p. 211); George H. Andries, Jr. (p. 212); Cari Wells (p. 213); the United States Army (p. 42); the United States Navy (pp. 202, 203); and the United States Air Force (pp. 12, 15–17, 20, 24 top, 54–56, 75, 90, 101, 128, 146, 153–154, 189 top, 192, 206).

Library of Congress Cataloguing-in-Publication Data

Strait, Jerry L., 1948–
  Vietnam War memorials.

  Includes index.
  1. Vietnamese Conflict, 1961–1975—Monuments—United States. 2. Vietnamese Conflict, 1961–1975—Monuments—United States—Pictorial works. I. Strait, Sandra S., 1948– . II. Title.
  DS559.825.S86   1988   959.704′3   87-46385

ISBN 0-89950-329-2 (50# acid-free natural paper) ∞

Printed in the United States of America.

McFarland   Box 611   Jefferson NC 28640

Table of Contents

Acknowledgments

Through the four years that we have worked on this project we have had terrific support from hundreds of individuals and local organizations. To these people who gave of their time to send us information and photos we owe our profound gratitude. We wish it were possible to recognize you all individually.

Our project was also supported by the following national organizations, who supplied information and printed our information requests in their publications:

American Gold Star Mothers, Inc.
American Legion
Amvets
Compuserve
Department of Defense
Disabled American Veterans
101st Airborne Division Association
Stars and Stripes
Static Line
United States Air Force
United States Army
United States Coast Guard
United States Marines
United States Navy
Veterans of Foreign Wars
Vet Centers
Vietnam Veterans of America
Vietnam Veterans Leadership Program
Vietnow

We are also very grateful to the nation's governors, their staffs, and their departments of veterans affairs, whose cooperation and assistance greatly aided our work.

During the many times of frustration and reluctance to continue this project, it was our family and friends that encouraged us. Special thanks must go to our parents and other family members, as well as Julio and Linda Gonzales, Fred Wilcox, Bill Laurie, Mary and Bernie Kephart, John and Chris Francis, Art and Charlotte Metcalfe, Mike Dotson and Ruth Ginsburg, Fred Patheiger, Don Moon of Drake University, Dann Hohn, Britt Small and "Festival," Mike Waldron, George Otto, and all our friends at the Des Moines Vet Center, whose assistance was invaluable.

Finally, we could not possibly have taken the time needed to research and write this book had it not been for the understanding and help of our children. They gave up many hours of "family time" to stuff envelopes, lick stamps, type addresses, take phone messages, and listen to us complain. Heather and Lori, our hope is that you and your generation may grow up in a world without war.

If I had to lose you, so you are now at peace and safe, triumphant in a hall of heroes. Your nation's flag gently embraces you as one day very soon my empty arms will, too. The medals on your chest you bravely won in the day of battle. They do not commemorate lost causes—for I do not see the enemy at our gates.

—Edward Patterson (Reprinted from the Sept.–Oct. 1984 edition of "The Screaming Eagle," a publication of the 101st Airborne Division Association.)

Show me the manner in which a nation or community cares for its dead and I will measure with mathematical exactness the tender sympathies of its people, their respect for the laws of the land, and their loyalty to high ideals.

—William Ewart Gladstone

Introduction

Because Jerry is a Vietnam combat veteran, we always enjoy attending veterans' functions with our family. It means a lot to us to be able to meet and talk with other people who share the sort of experiences that had such a profound impact on our lives. As we were driving to a Vietnam veterans memorial dedication in a nearby state, we discussed how much the memorials that were being built meant to the veterans and their families. We talked about how seeing and touching a monument helped vets to "come home," and in some way helped heal the wounds of the war and its aftermath.

It was then that we thought about the many vets still holding back, thinking that America didn't care about them. We wondered if there were some way we could show them that the people of our country do care, do respect them, and are showing it by the many monuments they are building.

From these thoughts the following pages were born. We had no idea where our efforts would lead, but thought we could at least put together a listing of ten or twenty monuments that we had heard about and see if there were more.

That was July of 1983. Since that time we have written hundreds of letters, made countless phone calls, and traveled as much as time and money would permit, to gather information about Vietnam memorials around the country.

Our project started by writing to the governors of every state requesting any information they had available on monuments in their states. From there the search led us to veterans affairs offices, veterans organizations, memorial committees, Vet Centers, individuals, and city and county government offices. The response and support we have received has been overwhelming, and we cannot thank those who helped us enough.

1

The memorials listed here number well over 300, and are located across the country, in every state, as well as overseas. We have also chosen to include monuments that honor veterans of all wars in which Americans fought, as long as Vietnam was included in the tribute. Many times an all-inclusive memorial was the best way for a community to pay tribute to their Vietnam veterans.

The individual monuments with photos and long descriptions are not necessarily the ones that we felt were the best, but the ones for which we were able to secure reasonably good photos and information. We listed every monument and location that we were able to confirm. For those communities having monuments that are not listed, we sincerely regret not being able to find them.

We should emphasize that this is not an "art" book. The photographs are not intended as works of art in themselves, nor do they pretend always to portray the memorials with the artistic sensibility many of them deserve. This book is simply our attempt to record the ever-multiplying manifestations of America's support and respect for her Vietnam veterans.

As our information grew, we were very surprised to find monuments built and dedicated to Vietnam veterans as early as 1966, and we are very pleased to say that they are still being built. Many are in the construction stages and others still in the planning stages.

It is our desire that this book help veterans and the public alike to overcome Vietnam. The sacrifices made by the living are diminished only by those of our brothers and sisters who didn't come home. We must make every effort to insure that they receive the respect they deserve and that they never be forgotten, whether they are known to have made the ultimate sacrifice or are among the more than 2,400 still missing in action.

Jerry and Sandy Strait

Alabama

Eufaula

In Southern Alabama, near the Chattahoochee River, is the small town of Eufaula. Command Sgt. Maj. William L. Nolin, Sr. (who proudly served two tours in Vietnam, Northern I Corps, 1965–66 and 1971–72), worked diligently with a committee to raise the funding from private contributions for Eufaula's beautiful Vietnam Veteran's Memorial Monument.

The memorial's focal point is a seven-foot column of Georgia marble topped by a noble bronze eagle, sculpted by Ken Bradford. Surrounding the column are four bronze plaques dedicating the art to all veterans of the Vietnam War.

Eufaula, Alabama: One of the four bronze plaques at the base of the Eufaula Vietnam Veteran's Memorial Monument.

3

Eufaula, Alabama: Two views of the Eufaula memorial, showing the bronze eagle in the center.

A two-day dedication celebration on May 28 & 29, 1983, included luncheons and a banquet with Gen. William C. Westmoreland, Medal of Honor recipients, and other distinguished guests. A skydiving exhibition by the Silver Wings of Ft. Benning, Georgia, and a parade complete with marching bands completed this very special weekend.

Other Alabama Memorials

Allgood: Memorial built of cement and moss rock.
Birmingham: World War I monument updated to include Vietnam.
Clanton: Pedestal with an eagle mounted on top.
Florence: Building with seventy-five-foot flag pole on top.
Montgomery: Memorial wall listing names of K.I.A.s and M.I.A.s.

Alaska

Byers Lake

The Alaska Veterans Memorial is located at Byers Lake, Mile 147.1 on the Parks Highway.

This unique memorial consists of five large concrete blocks representing each of the five branches of service, and a statue of two Alaskan servicemen, all placed in a parklike setting.

The dedication reads:

> We dedicate this quiet place to the remembrance of the veterans of Alaska who have served their country at home and throughout the world. We honor their heroism and dedication.

The plaques on each of the five blocks and the statue give an interesting history of Alaska's veterans, detailing their gallant participation in the defense of America's honor.

Other Alaska Memorials

Anchorage: Flagpole, 90 feet high.
Soldotna: Proposed monument in Soldotna Creek Park.

Opposite: *Byers Lake, Alaska: The Alaska Veterans Memorial, honoring veterans of all foreign wars, including Vietnam.*

Arizona

Phoenix

Through his work, noted sculptor Jasper d'Ambrosi has created an exceptional tribute to the courage and brotherhood that bonds Vietnam veterans together, then and now. His larger-than-life bronze statue of three soldiers is the focal point of the Arizona Vietnam Veterans Memorial in Wesley Bolin Plaza, part of the Capitol grounds in Phoenix. The statue is

Phoenix, Arizona: The Arizona Vietnam Veterans Memorial in Wesley Bolin Plaza.

8

Phoenix, Arizona: Detail of the statue in the Arizona memorial.

encircled by ten columns of black granite engraved with the names of the
613 Arizonans lost or missing in Vietnam.

A plaque on the memorial reads:

We the citizens of the state of Arizona dedicate this memorial to our men and women who served in the armed forces of the United States of America during the Vietnam War.

These granite columns symbolize the more than ten-year duration of that war. They bear the names of those who gave their lives and those who are still prisoners, or missing in action.

We honor them for their courage, dedication and sacrifice.

Let us always remember!

Dedicated November 9, 1985.

Arkansas

Blytheville Air Force Base

On December 18, 1974, nine former 97 BMW aircrew members who did not return from raids over North Vietnam were honored with the unveiling of an eight-foot stone monument erected in their memory at Blytheville Air Force Base in Arkansas. This monument has pictures of the nine men etched on its base and is topped by a replica of a B-52, created by TSgt. Paul C. Wert. The aircrew members listed were:

Col. Keith R. Heggen
Lt. Col. Donald L. Rissi
Maj. Bobby A. Kirby
Capt. Randall J. Craddock
Capt. Charles E. Darr
Capt. George B. Lockhart
Capt. Ronald D. Perry
Capt. Robert J. Thomas
SMSgt. Walter L. Ferguson

In his dedication speech, Lt. Gen. R.M. Hoban said:

The memorial we are dedicating today honors men—living and dead—who served during Strategic Air Command operations in Southeast Asia.... To the friends and families who waited at home for the return of our Arc Light crewmen, this memorial is a reminder of days of worry and uncertainty.... To all the people of SAC, this memorial will be a quiet reminder of a time when the men and women of Strategic Air Command did the job they were trained to do, in the manner in which it was meant to be done.

Blytheville Air Force Base also has a Freedom Tree and plaque located in front of the Base Chapel on Second Street. The dedication took place in 1973. Although the original tree died, the memorial plaque was moved next to a group of evergreen trees about five feet away. The present S.O.S. class has obtained a local tree and is staffing a ceremony for planting it.

The plaque reads:

> With the vision of universal freedom for all mankind this tree is dedicated to all P.O.W./M.I.A.s of Arkansas and all Prisoners of War and Missing in Action.

Little Rock

The Arkansas Vietnam Veterans' Memorial has a twofold purpose: to honor the sacrifice and courage of those who served and died in the war, and to focus public attention on the Vietnam veterans of the state. State Representative Doug Wood, in 1983, introduced legislation which appro-

Blytheville Air Force Base, Arkansas: Memorial to the crew of the Arc Light.

Little Rock, Arkansas: Two views of the Arkansas Vietnam Veterans' Memorial.

priated $150,000 for the project as well as establishing a committee to design the monument and authorizing the secretary of state to oversee the monument project.

The dedication of this fine state memorial took place March 7, 1987, on the State Capitol grounds in Little Rock. The names of 542 Arkansas residents who died in Vietnam, as well as 27 names of those still missing in action, are listed on the polished black granite panels on the memorial.

The memorial was designed by Steve Gartman, an architecture student at the University of Arkansas. It was selected from over 300 entries submitted in a statewide contest. Burt Taggart Associates did the architectural plans. Garver and Garver supplied the engineering drawings. 700,000 pounds of granite from Georgia and Pennsylvania were used in the memorial. Arkansas residents are very proud of their outstanding monument to Vietnam veterans.

California

Castle Air Force Base

Castle Air Force Base in California is the location of several memorials to Vietnam veterans. Two of these are the Memorial Parade Ground and the Linebacker Center.

The Memorial Parade Ground was dedicated in 1980 to all Air Force personnel assigned to Castle Air Force Base who gave their lives in support of the Air Force mission. It consists of an illuminated mariposite rock and year-round floral display containing the emblem of the 93rd Bombardment Wing. Another mariposite rock structure includes bronze memorial plaques. The entire parade ground, which is located in front of Base Headquarters, is encircled by flags of the fifty states set into a sidewalk.

Castle Air Force Base, California: Floral display on the Memorial Parade Ground.

Castle Air Force Base, California: Plaque at the Linebacker Center.

Castle Air Force Base, California: The Linebacker Center.

Linebacker Center is a flight simulator building dedicated September 28, 1981, to Air Force personnel who took part in Operation Linebacker. A beautiful wood and metal memorial plaque in the entrance hall of the building bears the following tribute to these heroic Americans:

Linebacker Center
Proudly dedicated to those who participated in Operation Linebacker 18–29 December 1972. The high altitude strategic B-52 bombing raids against North Vietnam ports were carried out against some of the most heavily defended targets in the history of aerial warfare. The heroic and valiant effort of SAC air and ground crew members in Operation Linebacker severely hampered North Vietnam's capabilities in waging war and led to the eventual release of U.S. Prisoners of War.

Fresno

Several local monuments to those who served during our nation's longest war have been built throughout the state of California. In Fresno, beside a quiet lake in Woodward Park, stands a lone boulder with a message of love inscribed on a bronze plaque. It reads:

IN MEMORIAM

To our 57,697 American
sons and daughters who lost
their tomorrows in the
"VIETNAM WAR"
1964 to 1975

by
AMERICANS WHO STILL CARE

July 4, 1981

Grass Valley

The Vietnam Veterans Memorial in Grass Valley is believed to be one of the first such monuments built in America. It was dedicated on Veterans Day, November 11, 1966, nine years before the end of our nation's longest war.

The memorial, located in Memorial Park, was dedicated to all American servicemen and women of the Vietnam War in the name of Gary Ames Miller, U.S.M.C. Gary was the first local serviceman to die in the war. The inscription on the bronze plaque reads, in part,

> All Americans owe an endless debt of gratitude to the gallant men and women of our armed services for preserving our way of life. A life endowed with justice, freedom, and democracy.

The base of the memorial is a round core of hard rock cut by diamond drills from the mines of Grass Valley. It was chosen to represent the hard rock gold mining of the area. This rock base sits on a poured concrete slab, washed to show the gravel, symbolic of the gravel mining also in this location in the early forty-niner days.

March Air Force Base

The tall, beautiful palm trees of March Air Force Base in California flank the sides of the white concrete memorial to Air Force personnel who participated in Operation Linebacker II. This operation was performed over North Vietnam in December of 1972. It proved to be strategically

Top: *Fresno, California: Memorial plaque in Woodward Park.* Bottom: *Grass Valley, California: Proud members of American Legion Post 130 encircle their Vietnam Veterans Memorial.*

March Air Force Base, California: Top: *Memorial for Air Force personnel of Operation Linebacker II.* Bottom: *A plaque on the Operation Linebacker II memorial.*

Marin County, California: Sculpture, "The Brothers," which sits atop the Marin County Korean/Vietnam Memorial.

important to the later release of American P.O.W.s. The three-foot-high structures contain several plaques and nameplates of Air Force, wing, and base commanders, as well as names four officers listed as M.I.A. and five as P.O.W. as a result of the operation. The monument is located on the southwest side of the base parade ground and was dedicated in 1974.

Marin County

The time spent waiting and praying, hoping for news and yet dreading the thought of what that news might be, wore heavily on the families of the men and women who served in Vietnam. The 365-day tour seemed like an eternity to those who waited at home as well as those who served. One mother, Mary Beeson, of Yountville, California, especially felt the pain of waiting for her son, as it reminded her of the thirty months she had once waited for her young husband to return from World War II.

In 1967, to help endure this anguish, Mary began to sculpt a small bust of a scene she'd seen in a media photo. It was of two soldiers, a white infantryman who'd lost a leg in battle being helped by a black comrade. She called her work "The Brothers."

Years later this small sculpture became the model for the life-size statue which was dedicated on Veterans Day, 1985, as part of the combined Korean/Vietnam Memorial of Marin County, California. Retired Army Lt. Col. Walter Filler led the Marin County United Veterans Council's fundraising efforts.

The marble base of the statue bears the names of Marin County residents who lost their lives in the war, and the following words:

> Dedicated with thanks by the people of Marin County, November 11, 1985, to all who served this country in Korea and Vietnam, and sacrificed so much that others might be free. For those who gave their lives there is no tomorrow. May their souls rest in peace.

Norton Air Force Base

A tall evergreen was planted in 1978 as a Freedom Tree in memory of our prisoners of war and missing in action. The tree and nearby dedication plaque are located on the south lawn of the Headquarters building at Norton Air Force Base in California. The inscription on the plaque reads:

> The Freedom Tree
>
> With the vision of universal freedom
> for all mankind
> this tree is dedicated to
> Military Airlift Command POW/MIAs

and all
Prisoners of War
and
Missing in Action

Sacramento

More than any other state, California gave of its very best, its youth, to fight for the freedom of those oppressed in Southeast Asia. Over 5,800 Californians were killed or are still missing as a result of that noble effort. There are at least 350,000 California veterans who served in Vietnam. To honor these many residents, citizens have formed a commission to raise $2,000,000 to construct a memorial on the State Capitol grounds, just east of the Capitol building, in Sacramento. The commission hopes to complete construction by May 30, 1988.

Bob Hope, a longtime California resident, is the chairman of the memorial fund campaign's "Blue Ribbon Committee." He serves along with such other well-known people as President Gerald R. Ford, General William Westmoreland, Governor George Deukmejian, Mayor Tom Bradley, singer Lee Greenwood, and comedian Fred Travalena. They hope to call statewide attention to the campaign.

The winning design for the California Vietnam Veterans Memorial was conceived by Michael Larson and Thomas Chytrowski of San Francisco. In its shape, which consists of broken concentric circular walls, it represents a reflection of life. The walls form a drum with four entrances at the four points of the compass.

One of the largest Vietnam memorials, it covers over 3,750 square feet, with the innermost circular wall being twenty-two feet in diameter and two feet thick. The main entrance is the southern one, which is marked by a polished granite map of South Vietnam engraved in the walkway.

The focal point of the memorial is the bronze figure of a nineteen-year-old combat veteran. He is shown seated on his helmet, reading a welcome letter from home. The four inner walls that surround him have niches which are each mounted with a thematic bronze bas-relief. There are also three smaller bas-relief panels on the sides of each niche. All of the bas-reliefs are taken from selected combat photographs. They follow the themes of the emotional impact on individual soldiers. One shows the nurses who served in Vietnam as well.

The names of the 5,822 Californians killed or missing are engraved on

Top: *Norton Air Force Base, California: Freedom Tree and dedicatory plaque.* Bottom: *Sacramento, California: Model for the California Vietnam Veterans Memorial on the grounds of the State Capitol.*

twenty-two granite panels mounted on the outer surfaces of the inner walls. Each name is alphabetized under the person's hometown. The commission decided this would make the memorial a community tribute as well as a state memorial. A "treasury" will stand at the rear of the memorial. It will contain a time capsule containing a list of all who contributed to the memorial fund. Placed on top of this will be a bronze sculpture of a pair of boots, a helmet, and a cartridge belt.

Linda J. McClenahan serves as chairperson for the California Vietnam Veterans Memorial Commission. She reports a massive, statewide effort is underway, with several communities planning unique fundraising events, including everything from $100-a-plate dinners to a '50s and '60s sock hop. Numerous corporate contributions have been made ranging from $100 to $20,000. Also, more than two-thirds of the funds raised have come from individual donors. A model of the memorial is being transported throughout the state to fundraising events by American Red Ball agents. The commission is making every effort to complete its plans for an outstanding memorial to pay tribute to its heroes, the Vietnam veterans.

Sacramento River Bridge

The Sacramento River Bridge on Interstate I-5 at Sacramento, near the airport, was dedicated to all veterans killed in Vietnam. This project was sponsored by the Camellia Amvets Post #165 of Sacramento and designed by Ralph Grace. The site was donated by the state of California and constructed by the people of the six-county area. A plaque on the bridge, from the Catholic Cemeteries, Diocese of Sacramento, reads:

> Prayer
> Dedicated to all of the servicemen who have given up so much for the war in Vietnam.
> May they rest in peace forever in the bosom of our Lord.

Sanger

The average age of the American serviceman in Vietnam was nineteen. Many never lived past that tender age. Specialist 4 Danny Appleton, U.S.A.F., had barely celebrated his nineteenth birthday when he was killed in action, defending the liberty of others in a faraway jungle.

Top: *Sacramento River Bridge, California: Plaques announcing the dedication of this bridge to Vietnam veterans.* Bottom: *Sanger, California: Town memorial to area Vietnam veterans.*

His name, as well as the names of many other area citizens, is listed on the massive stone monument in the small California town of Sanger, just east of Fresno. The monument was dedicated June 1, 1983.

Danny's mother, Jewell E. Appleton, is very proud of her son and the contributions to our country that he was able to make in his short lifetime.

Santa Barbara

"This Vietnam Veterans Living Memorial will be a place to remember, to reflect, to honor, and to find solace," according to Gregg Steele, chair of the committee to build a memorial in Santa Barbara, California. A 1,200-foot trail in Las Positas Park will be planted with ninety-six redwood trees, each one commemorating a resident of Santa Barbara County who lost his life in Southeast Asia. These young people came from several areas around the county and served in all branches of the armed services.

Ten sandstone walls will be inlaid with serpentine marble plaques bearing the names of those lost or missing in the war. Both veterans and non-veterans are involved in this countywide effort.

Whittier

The Whittier Memorial Association of Whittier, California, was started by two Gold Star Mothers who felt that their community should have its own veterans memorial. The association spent four years soliciting funds for the sundial-topped monument, which is located on the grounds of the City Hall. They dedicated it in the American Bicentennial year, 1976.

The sides of the base are engraved with the names of people killed or missing in action in World War I, World War II, Korea, and Vietnam. The monument is encircled by concrete benches and tall cypress trees that make it a quiet place of personal reflection.

Vacaville

One of a unique pair of bronze eagles perches atop the seven-foot-high Solano County Vietnam War Memorial in Vacaville, California. The other eagle can be found at the Lyndon B. Johnson ranch in Texas. The memorial was built by the Brotherhood of Vietnam Veterans of Vacaville through fundraising projects. Over 1,000 people attended the emotional May 26, 1986, dedication.

Whittier, California: Memorial to veterans of World War I, World War II, Korea, and Vietnam.

Vacaville, California: The Solano County Vietnam War Memorial.

Other California Memorials

San Francisco: Display of flags with bronze plaque surrounded by cypress trees.

San Jose: Proposed monument to be built by Nationalist Vietnamese organization.

Santa Ana: Orange County Veterans Memorial. Four free-standing pillars with bronze plaque. Located in the Santa Ana Civic Center Plaza.

Colorado

Denver

The Mile High City of Denver will be the home of Colorado's State Veterans Memorial. The Colorado Tribute to Veterans Fund, Inc., was formed in May of 1983 as an all-volunteer, private corporation. Their goal is to raise a projected $460,000 to build a tribute to commemorate the service and sacrifice of all veterans, with special recognition of the 5,400 Coloradoans who died in Vietnam, Korea, World War II and World War I.

The site of the proposed memorial is the west grounds of the State Capitol. There will also be a permanent display of the Colorado War Dead Honor Roll and Journal of Contributors in the west entrance of the State Capitol.

The striking design for the memorial was submitted by the architectural firm of Johnson-Hopson and Partners of Denver. The team leaders are Robert W. Root and Richard C. Farley. The thirty-foot-tall granite tower is topped by a pyramid of translucent glass that will be illuminated at night and serve as a beacon. The granite reflecting pool will be fifty-eight feet long and fourteen feet wide. The surrounding walkways will consist of Colorado red sandstone and granite bands.

After the annual Denver Memorial Day Parade in 1987, in conjunction with the fund raising, a reading of the 5,400 names on the Colorado War Dead Honor Roll took place. Because of the massive crowds in attendance, the reading took over eight-and-one-half hours. Early that morning, small American flags were placed in twenty-two rows, each 125 feet long, on the west side of the State Capitol to represent the war dead.

With the motto "Colorado Cares," the fund hopes to raise the remainder of the money needed in the near future. As of May 1, 1987, they had collected $200,000, or almost half of the projected amount.

Opposite: *Denver: Drawing of proposed Colorado State Veterans Memorial.*

Connecticut

New Britain

"The sacrifices of those who fought and died for the principles of liberty, self-determination, and freedom in Vietnam are a source of pride and honor for this nation.... It is important that we recognize that the veterans of the Vietnam War, indeed, reflect the commitment to freedom that is the very foundation of this democracy...." So stated William J. McNamara, mayor of New Britain, Connecticut, in his official proclamation marking the dedication of their Vietnam Veterans Memorial on November 11, 1983.

Stamford

It took fifteen years for the Stamford, Connecticut, Veterans Memorial Monument to finally become a reality on November 13, 1977. Both private and municipal funds were raised over the years to cover the total cost of around $140,000. The original designs were by Alfred Yaeger, a designer for Rock of Ages Memorials. Modifications were eventually made in the designs, and were prepared for the craftsmen, by Eugene Brusetti. The superb sculpture work was done by Frank Marchini and Alcide Fantoni.

The entire memorial honoring World War II, Korea, and Vietnam veterans of Stamford is made up of four massive, twenty-two-foot, blue-gray granite monoliths which stand on a round platform. They encircle a time capsule unit, topped by a bronze statue of a World War I soldier that was taken from another site and restored. Each of the four monoliths is unique in design. Two of them have carved figures and quotes from Abraham

Top: *New Britain, Connecticut: The New Britain Vietnam Veterans Memorial.* Bottom: *West Hartford, Connecticut: Stone and bronze monument commemorating West Hartford men killed in Vietnam.*

Lincoln and Lawrence Binyon. One stone contains a list of 271 names of area residents killed in the three wars. The final stone is inscribed with President Franklin D. Roosevelt's "Four Freedoms": Freedom of Speech, Freedom of Worship, Freedom from Want, and Freedom from Fear. The impressive monument is certainly a source of pride for the city of Stamford.

West Hartford

Members and friends of Hannon-Hatch V.F.W. Post 9929 of West Hartford, Connecticut, paid homage to sixteen men from their town who died in Southeast Asia. They remembered them with a large stone and bronze monument located in front of the Elmwood Community Center on New Britain Avenue. This quiet reminder was erected in 1983.

Other Connecticut Memorials

Dedham: Seven-foot section of marble with marble wings, inscribed with drawings of equipment and symbols for P.O.W./M.I.A.s. Names of K.I.A.s will be inscribed. Dedicated May 26, 1986.

Wallingford: (1) Black stone monument listing names of citizens killed in Vietnam, as well as names of those who served. Located in Dutton Park and dedicated November 11, 1985. (2) Stone and plaque listing names of war dead. Located in Pragman Park and dedicated in 1984.

West Hartford: Several banner-type memorials located around the town.

Willimantic: Stone plaque with names of those killed in Vietnam. Located in Soldiers, Sailors, and Marines Park. Dedicated February 8, 1982.

Windsor Locks: Granite wall inscribed to honor local Vietnam vets that served. Located on the front lawn of Memorial Hall on Main Street, dedicated May 1976.

Other Memorials are located in these cities:
Bridgeport
East Hartford
Manchester
New London
Old Mystic
Torrington

Delaware

Wilmington

Seventeen M-16 rifles inserted barrels down, with helmets placed on the rifle butts and jungle boots alongside, marked the seventeen campaigns of the Vietnam War on Veterans Day 1983 in Wilmington, Delaware. This was all part of the dedication ceremonies for the New Castle County Vietnam Veterans Memorial. The powerful nine-foot bronze statue, entitled "Vietnam," was created by Charles Parks of Wilmington. A solemn look of disbelief crosses the face of the lone black soldier as he carries the lifeless body of his white brother. Beneath his feet, on a tall brick mound, are the names of 166 Delaware residents who lost their lives in Southeast Asia.

Other Delaware Memorials

Highway I-495: Dedicated as the Vietnam Veterans Memorial Highway

Wilmington, Delaware: The New Castle County Vietnam Veterans Memorial is topped by this bronze sculpture, entitled "Vietnam."

District of Columbia

So many things have been written about the National Vietnam Veterans Memorial in Washington, D.C., that it is very hard to describe it. We should say that "The Wall," as veterans everywhere refer to it, means many things to many people – perhaps something different to each one of the millions who have now experienced it.

First of all, it is strikingly unique in comparison to the hundreds of other memorials in Washington, D.C. It does not seek to glorify war in any way. It serves rather to reflect the viewer's own thoughts, like a mirror to one's soul, with its highly polished black granite face. As you look at the wall you see yourself in reflection, mingled with the names of the dead and missing.

Washington, D.C.: Visitors line up to see the Vietnam Veterans Memorial.

Washington, D.C.: Honoring the dead at the National Vietnam Veterans Memorial.

The most powerful aspect of "The Wall" is the massive list of names. The names of over 58,000 Americans are listed on its face. Americans who never came home from the war in Vietnam; never grew up or grew older; never again saluted the flag, or hugged their mothers, or kissed their sweethearts, or reached out to their fathers. The average age of these young people was only nineteen.

On April 27, 1979, the Vietnam Veterans Memorial Fund was incorporated by a group of Vietnam veterans in Washington, D.C., led by Jan Scruggs, a wounded veteran who had long dreamed of a national tribute to those lost in the war. Robert Doubek and John Wheeler, along with many others, worked on the Vietnam Veterans Memorial Fund until the memorial was finally ready for dedication on November 13, 1982.

The original design for the memorial was submitted by Maya Ying Lin of Athens, Ohio. "The Wall" itself is actually two walls, one pointing west to the Lincoln Memorial and one pointing east to the Washington Monument, meeting at the apex or center. At the apex, the walls are slightly over ten feet high, and then each one tapers down to a point, giving the appearance of a wide, slim "V" from above. Miss Lin designed it so that the entire memorial is actually below street level, the earth behind it having been cut out from a hillside. As you walk along the sidewalk in front of it, you go down an incline to the apex, then back up again to street level. This gives an added feeling of solitude.

The names are arranged in chronological order by the person's date of death, starting at the apex with 1959, going east through about summer of 1968, then starting again at the tip of the west wall and going back to the apex, ending at 1975. In this way the memorial is a look at history. Names can be found in two ways, either by the date of death, or by looking in the alphabetical directories available at all times near the memorial.

In January of 1982, plans were developed to add a figurative statue and a large flagstaff to the site of the National Vietnam Veterans Memorial. At that time, many citizens desired an additional tribute at the site to those who survived the war. It was decided that the statue would symbolize the devotion to country of, and sacrifices made by, the American soldier in Vietnam. Noted Washington sculptor Frederick Hart was chosen to design and create a sculpture that would meet that need.

The life-size, bronze sculpture of three infantrymen was completed and installed on the southwest hillside which faces "The Wall." It clearly depicts the sense of unity and bonds of loyalty among the American fighting men. The dedication of this tremendous work was held in November of 1984, with thousands in attendance. President Reagan gave the dedication speech, wherein he recognized the outstanding devotion and service of all Vietnam veterans to this country.

The bronze figure of a screaming eagle landing swiftly but silently tops the 101st Airborne Division Association Memorial near the entrance to Arlington National Cemetery. The monument and nearby engraved walls

Washington, D.C.: This bronze sculpture was added to the site of the National Vietnam Veterans Memorial in 1984.

recall the many campaigns of both World War II and Vietnam in which paratroopers of the 101st Airborne Division participated. The division was well represented in the jungles of Vietnam; over 20,000 battle casualties from that war alone are recognized on the tall granite stone. The association proudly welcomes all former Screaming Eagles back to the nest with annual Memorial Day services at this monument as well as "The Wall" in Washington.

Arlington, Virginia: The memorial of the 101st Airborne Division is topped by a bronze eagle, representing the division's nickname, "The Screaming Eagles."

The interment of the Unknown Serviceman of Vietnam, which took place May 28, 1984, paid full and final tribute to a soldier "known but to God," who now represents all persons who died in the war. A full honor state funeral, during which President Ronald Reagan presented the Congressional Medal of Honor to the Unknown, was conducted in the Memorial Amphitheater at Arlington National Cemetery.

Top: *Arlington, Virginia: The Tomb of the Unknown Soldiers. The casket of the Unknown Serviceman of Vietnam awaits interment.* Bottom: *Arlington, Virginia: The funeral for the Unknown Serviceman of Vietnam.*

Arlington, Virginia: The United States Marine Corps War Memorial.

After the funeral, the casket was moved to the Plaza at the Tomb of the Unknown Soldiers for a twenty-one-gun salute, wreath presentation by President Reagan, and the sounding of Taps. As the United States Army Band played "America the Beautiful," the casket flag was folded and presented to the president. The flag, along with the Medal of Honor and the Purple Heart, are now on display at the Memorial Amphitheater at Arlington.

The United States Marine Corps War Memorial in Arlington, Virginia, was dedicated on November 10, 1954, to all Marines, past, present, and future, who have given or will give their lives to their country.

The memorial reverently depicts the second flag-raising on Mount Suribachi, Iwo Jima, a proud moment to all Marines. The bronze statue, created by Felix DeWeldon, was modeled after the famous Joe Rosenthal photograph. This imposing war memorial stands seventy-eight feet high overall, with the figures being thirty-two feet tall, and was paid for entirely by Marines, Marine Reservists, friends of the Marine Corps and members of the Naval Service.

The Sunset Parade, complete with dress-uniformed precision drill and concert by the Marine Drum and Bugle Corps, is performed at the memorial each Tuesday at 6:00 p.m. from June through August.

I don't go off to war,
so they say,
I'm a woman.

Who then
has worn my boots?
And whose memories are these,
of youths suffering? Of
blood and burns, of their
tears and their cries?

I'm a woman
and I've tasted man's war.
Our war. And
he knows that I
love him in
no greater way
than to share in his life
or his death.

What are the rules?
Man or woman,
we are prey
to suffer and survive together.

Please don't forget me.
I've been through war's hell
and if only you will listen,
I've a story
of those chosen
to sacrifice for us all.

Diane Carlson Evans
1983

The Vietnam Women's Memorial Project, headed by Diane Carlson Evans and Donna Marie Boulay, commissioned noted Minneapolis sculptor Rodger M. Brodin to create a statue honoring women's role in the war in Vietnam. The project was originally known as the Vietnam Nurses Memorial Project, but was later expanded to represent the exceptional contributions made by all women who served in Southeast Asia. When completed, the plans are to position the statue near "The Wall" in Washington, D.C.

Opposite, left: *Washington, D.C.: This statue, when completed, will be placed near "The Wall" to honor the women who served in Southeast Asia.* Opposite, right: *Facial detail of the statue.*

Washington, D.C.: This photograph of Sharon Lane, the only American servicewoman killed as a result of enemy action during the Vietnam War, is shown in the Department of Defense display honoring women in the armed forces, located in the Pentagon.

Opposite: Washington, D.C.: Special display in the Pentagon honoring women's contributions to the armed forces.

It is not widely known, but there are eight women listed on "The Wall." They were all nurses, and they all died serving their country. They were:

Eleanor Grace Alexander
Pamela Dorothy Donovan
Carol Ann Drazba
Annie Ruth Graham
Elizabeth A. Jones
Mary T. Klinker
Sharon Anne Lane
Hedwig Diane Orlowski

On November 16, 1983, the Department of Defense dedicated a special display in the Pentagon honoring the many contributions made by the women who serve in the armed forces of the United States. It is located in the "A Ring" (the innermost hallway of the Pentagon) between corridors 6 and 7 on the second floor. The display consists of ten cases and a wall display of photographs and artwork relating to women in the military.

Case 7 of the display contains a photo and biography of First Lieutenant Sharon Lane, Army Nurse Corps. Lieutenant Lane was one of about 7,500 women who served in Southeast Asia, most of whom were Army, Navy, or Air Force nurses. In all, eight women died while on duty in Vietnam, most in aircraft crashes. Lieutenant Lane was the only American servicewoman killed as a result of enemy action during the Vietnam War. Her biography in the lower lefthand corner of the display case reads:

Sharon A. Lane

First Lieutenant Sharon A. Lane, Army Nurse Corps, was the only American servicewoman killed as a result of enemy action during the Vietnam War. She died on June 8, 1969, of wounds received during a rocket attack while on duty at the 312th Evacuation Hospital in Chu Lai, Republic of Vietnam. In November 1969, Fitzsimons General Hospital in Denver, Colorado, where she first served as an Army nurse, dedicated the Lane Recovery Suite in her memory. In 1973, a life-size statue of Lieutenant Lane was unveiled at her alma matter, Aultman Hospital, in her home town of Canton, Ohio.

Florida

Deland

On Veterans Day, 1983, Deland, Florida, welcomed home its Vietnam veterans with the dedication of a large African granite monument built through the efforts of the Sunrise Kiwanis Club and other concerned citizens. The ceremony was complete with a fly-over by four Cobra gunship helicopters, the ones so often seen in the battles of Vietnam.

Vietnam veteran John Allen chaired the memorial committee for the

Deland, Florida: Vietnam Veterans gather for the dedication of the Deland Vietnam Veterans Monument.

IN APPRECIATION
TO MEMBERS OF
OUR ARMED FORCES
WHO SERVED IN
VIET-NAM.

DELAND SUNRISE KIWANIS
1983

Deland, Florida: The Deland Vietnam Veterans Monument.

Kiwanis. At the dedication in Veterans Park, he spoke of the individual sacrifices made by all who served during the war. He said that the individual efforts of all Americans contribute to our strength as a nation.

Dunedin, Florida: The Dunedin High School Memorial Stadium.

Dunedin

The community of Dunedin, Florida, a suburb of the Clearwater–St. Petersburg area, is the site of one of the earliest memorials to Vietnam veterans. The Dunedin High School Memorial Stadium was dedicated September 15, 1968, with marble plaques bearing the names of thirteen area servicemen who died in Vietnam. Since that time, nine Honor Roll plaques have been added with the names of men and women who served in the armed services during the war. Mr. E.J. Flowers and other interested citizens led the community in the effort to recognize their veterans.

The original plaques read:

> Dunedin Memorial Stadium is hereby dedicated by the citizens of Dunedin in memory of our loved ones who have served courageously with valor, honor, and dignity in the Armed Forces of their country during the Vietnam conflict, to insure the Freedom of Mankind, thus making a better world in which to live.
>
> In hallowed memory by a grateful city, to those who gave their all that those freedoms laid down by the Constitution of the United States will be preserved for all who shall so seek.

Top: *Dunedin, Florida: The Dunedin V.F.W. Veterans Memorial as it appeared when dedicated in 1970.* Bottom: *Dunedin, Florida: The eagle was added to the top of the Dunedin monument in 1972.*

The early construction of this monument, even in the height of the war, is evidence that Americans were paying tribute to their soldiers, if not necessarily to the war.

Another memorial in Dunedin is the V.F.W. Veterans Memorial. This large monument is composed of a total of fifty-two stones, one from each state, Washington, D.C., and the Panama Canal Zone. Over a period of six years, the stones were collected, one from each of the V.F.W. state headquarters.

The monument was dedicated to all veterans on August 23, 1970. An eagle was later added to the top in 1972. The dedication plaque reads:

> Dedicated to recall in the minds of all men those Americans who did not ask, but who have repeatedly served under this country's flag to their fullest whenever the cause of freedom and democracy has been threatened anywhere in the world.

Eglin Air Force Base

On May 29, 1968, a twenty-three-acre, freshwater man-made lake, stocked with rainbow trout, bass, and bream fish, was dedicated to Air Force personnel who lost their lives in Southeast Asia. Named Memorial Lake, it is located on the main base of Eglin Air Force Base in Florida. It is surrounded by biking trails, as well as picnic and wildlife areas.

The dedication ceremonies in 1968 took place before the large white monument which sits on high ground overlooking the lake. During the ceremony, two Silver Stars for gallantry in Southeast Asia were presented to Lt. Col. John Reddoch and Maj. James G. Wyatt, by Maj. Gen. Andrew J. Kinney, commander of the Air Proving Ground Center. The 1968 dedication date makes this one of the earliest, as well as loveliest, of the Vietnam veterans memorials.

Eglin Air Force Base is also the site of seven other unique memorial tributes to Vietnam veterans. They are all located on Air Force Auxiliary Field No. 6, Hurlburt Field.

The first was dedicated in May of 1978 to all men and women who served their country in Southeast Asia. It consists of three stone podiums with attached bronze plaques, set among a lovely configuration of shrubbery. It was in memoriam to the 52 Spectre–16th Special Operations

Eglin Air Force Base, Florida: Memorial Lake, dedicated to Air Force personnel killed in Southeast Asia.

Top: *Eglin Air Force Base, Florida: Memorial to the 52 Spectre–16th Special Operations Squadron. Bottom: Eglin Air Force Base, Florida: Mounted A1E Skyraider dedicated to American and South Vietnamese aircrew members.*

Eglin Air Force Base, Florida: Mounted aircraft displays honoring American and South Vietnamese aircrews. Top: *The UH-IP "Huey."* Bottom: *The A26.*

Squadron. One plaque reads, in part, "In war's grim hour that tested all, among the first, they heard the call. They fought for peace with honor."

The other six tributes are mounted aircraft displays, dedicated to the American and South Vietnamese crews that served in them during the war. They consist of the following:

The *A1E Skyraider*, a single-engine fighter bomber, dedicated May 30, 1972. The dedication plaque reads, in part, "This aircraft memorial is dedicated to all USAF personnel and our fellow Vietnamese Airmen who flew A1Es in the Southeast Asia conflict. It also commemorates all those who selflessly gave their lives in combat to preserve the ideals that we and freedom loving people throughout the world so highly cherish."

The *UH-1P "Huey,"* flown by the men of project "Lucky Tiger" and the 14th Air Commando Wing "Green Hornets," dedicated in October 1981. The dedication plaque reads, in part, "This aircraft memorial honors the tradition, courage and sacrifice of the personnel who maintained and flew Special Operations helicopters in the defense of freedom."

The *C-123 twin-engine cargo plane* was used extensively in many roles, including tactical airlift, aerial spraying, night illumination, and sensor missions. All of these complemented the Air Commando/Special Operations Mission. The tribute was dedicated October 11, 1981. Part of the dedication plaque reads, "This aircraft memorial is dedicated to those who maintained and flew the C-123 in the defense of freedom."

The *A-26 twin-engine medium night bomber* used by the Air Commandos was dedicated on July 4, 1980. Part of the dedication plaque reads, "This aircraft memorial is dedicated to all USAF personnel who flew A-26s in World War II, Korea, and Southeast Asia. It especially commemorates all those aircrew members who gave their lives flying in defense of the United States and freedom loving people everywhere."

Mounted *Cessna 0-1's* represent the many forward air controllers used in Vietnam for aerial surveillance and in spotting targets. The following names of aircrafts are mentioned on the dedication plaques: "Nail, Rustic, Covey, Raven, Crickett, Gumbie, Cutie, Sunday, Lopez, Helix, Jake, Hammer, Spike, Rash, Rage, Snort, and Bluebat."

Although no monument is attached to it, there is an *AC-47 "Spooky"* or *"Puff the Magic Dragon"* gunship, which should serve to remind us all of the brave crews that served in them.

Hialeah, Florida: Scenes from the David H. McDonald Memorial Park.

Hialeah

The names on "The Wall" in Washington, D.C., are so much more than just names. They represent real people who led important lives: important to those around them, those who loved and needed them.

One of those names is David H. McDonald of Hialeah, Florida. David was important to his family, his friends, his fiancée, and especially to the many, many children who looked up to this fine young man. He had formed close bonds of friendship with teenagers and younger children alike through his job with the Recreation Department at O'Quinn Park. He was studying to be a physical education teacher at a local college and looking forward to spending his life helping children grow and learn. When he entered service and left for the war in Vietnam, he kept up the friendship with the children of O'Quinn Park by writing to them often, advising them and encouraging them always to do their best. His death on April 4, 1969, saddened and shocked the community and the children.

The citizens of Hialeah decided to dedicate a newly built park to Sergeant McDonald after he was killed. The sixteen-acre park has since been updated to include a huge fountain with a forty-foot water spout, a pier, eleven pavilions, a large playground area, and many beautiful coconut and palm trees. The park is a fitting tribute to someone who led such an important, if brief, life.

Miami

Tropical Park, at 7900 S.W. 40th Street in Miami, is a picturesque setting for the five-sided white pillar dedicated to veterans of five wars: Spanish American, World War I, World War II, Korea, and Vietnam. Each side of the pillar is inscribed with the emblem of one of the branches of service. Completing the memorial are five benches representing each of the wars. This novel monument was built through the combined donations of civic and veterans' organizations, as well as caring veterans and citizens.

North Miami

The North Miami Veterans Memorial is located at 13250 N.E. 8th Avenue. It consists of a raised half-circle of walls with bronze plaques dedicating the memorial to veterans of all wars.

Orlando

At least five high schools in Orlando, Florida, have memorials to former students who died defending their country. They are Bishop Moore

Miami, Florida: Two views of the Miami Veterans Memorial. Five benches (note Vietnam bench in bottom photo) represent five foreign wars.

North Miami, Florida: Two views of the North Miami Veterans Memorial.

Orlando, Florida: Vietnam Memorial at Boone High School, engraved with the names of Boone students who died in the war.

High School, Boone High School, Colonial High School, Edgewater High School, and Maynard Evans High School. For the most part, these memorials were built through funds raised by the students themselves.

A typical story is that of the Boone High School Monument. In May of 1985, a striking black granite memorial was dedicated to the thirty-two Boone High students who had lost their lives in the war in Vietnam. The memorial, donated by former student Mitch Gazil, was the direct result of two years of work by student Wil Houseman. Writing a theme on the Vietnam veterans' homecoming had sparked Houseman's interest, and he began a crusade to see that the Vietnam veterans of his school were honored as other veterans had been.

The City of Orlando has dedicated a park "to the men and women of the 306 Bomb Wing and the citizens of the Orlando area in memory of the long-standing, close relationship which existed between the members of the USAF Strategic Air Command and this community between 1957 and 1974."

Top: *Orlando, Florida: Visitors enjoying a park dedicated to veterans by the City of Orlando.* Bottom: *Orlando, Florida: A B52D bomber serves as a memorial in the park.*

In the park stands a proud veteran of Vietnam, a retired B52D bomber. The dedication plaque on the observation stand tells the story behind this seasoned warrior:

> This veteran bomber is the last of its breed to be retired from duty. Her final flight from Carswell Air Force Base, Fort Worth, Texas, to Orlando was made on February 20th, 1984, twenty-two years after the D model first joined the operational roster of Strategic Air Command.
>
> The black paint of Air Force 687 attests to many combat stories in the Viet Nam conflict; the wrinkled skin to many low-altitude training flights for the strategic mission; and the massive silhouette to the thousands of hours standing alert that epitomize the SAC dedication: PEACE IS OUR PROFESSION.
>
> From 1963 to 1974 the 306th Bombardment Wing at McCoy Air Force Base (now Orlando International Airport) was equipped with these B52D's. They memorialize these eleven years of exemplary joint effort, coordination and friendship between the military and the community, and our venerable war and peace bird, like many of those who flew and cared for her, has made Central Florida home in testimony to a lasting bond.

The Orange County Vietnam Memorial and Courtyard, located in the Orange County Civic Center on International Drive in Orlando, was erected in an original pyramid design. The dedication plaque reads:

> This memorial is dedicated to those brave Americans from Orange County who paid the ultimate sacrifice for their country while in Vietnam.
>
> The courtyard in which the memorial lies is dedicated to all those brave Americans who served in Vietnam.

Palm Harbor

Each year until 1986 the sixth, seventh, and eighth graders of Palm Harbor Middle School, in Palm Harbor, Florida, built their own "Wall of Remembrance" on Veterans Day. The names of the students' friends and relatives who served in the armed forces were listed on the wall. Tony George, American Industries teacher, helped the students to design, construct, and paint the wall. The social studies teachers helped the students compile the names to put on the wall.

In 1986, a permanent wall was built of plywood and pine studs, by Mr. George and the students. Since then, the students display new names for

Palm Harbor, Florida: Students of the Palm Harbor Middle School honor friends and relatives in the service with their Wall of Remembrance.

the new student body each year. The social studies teachers help compile the names, which are then printed on white poster board and attached to the permanent wall.

It is a tradition that during Veterans Day ceremonies, the National Anthem is played as the students pass by and place flowers on or near the wall. They search for names they are proud to remember. In this way they can become personally involved in honoring their nation's heroes.

South Seminole County

South Seminole County V.F.W. Post 8207 erected a fine monument to veterans of all wars. It serves as a base for their flag. The inscription reads:

> In memory of the men and women who served their country in the armed forces of the United States of America during times of conflict on foreign lands, skies and seas. May their valor and honor forever be remembered.

South Seminole County, Florida: V.F.W. monument to veterans of all wars.

Tallahassee

Florida's state monument, the Vietnam Era Veterans Memorial, built near the Old Capitol in Tallahassee, is an exceptionally impressive commemoration. It consists of two forty-foot pylons with a huge American flag draped between them.

Floridians are proud to report that the 1984 State Legislature set aside over $460,000 to fund this unique memorial, designed by James R. Kolb and dedicated Veterans Day 1985. The names of Florida residents who died in or are missing because of the war are inscribed on the inside polished stone of the pylons.

Tallahassee, Florida: The Vietnam Era Veterans Memorial is the state memorial of Florida.

Other Florida Memorials

Fort Lauderdale: Life-size statue of a soldier with a plaque listing names of 159 soldiers killed. Located in War Memorial Auditorium. (May be relocated.) Dedicated Memorial Day 1972.

Georgia

Hull

Many different time periods have been used as the duration of the Vietnam War. "The Wall" in Washington, D.C., recognizes 1959–1975. Other sources say 1961–1975. On a farm near Hull, Georgia, a tall granite monument lists the duration of the war as 1945–1975, a full thirty years.

John Snyder, the farm owner, felt this was more appropriate, and historians may very well agree with him. His memorial was dedicated April 7, 1985. An annual Vietnam veterans campout is held at the sight, which is known as L.Z. Friendly. (In Vietnam, L.Z. stood for landing zone, a clearing in which helicopters could land.)

Beneath the engraved years 1945–1975 is the simple statement, "Lest We Forget."

Snellville

On May 4, 1985, a crowd of over 6,000 was present to witness the unveiling of the Vietnam Memorial in Snellville, Georgia. The lighting of the eternal flame atop the monument concluded the dedication ceremony, which featured guest speaker United States Senator Mack Mattingly, a twenty-one-gun salute, the playing of taps, and a missing-in-action fly-over provided by the 116th Tactical Fighter Wing. The proud sponsors of this seven-foot-tall, ten-ton monument carved from native Georgia blue-gray granite were the Snellville Jaycees.

Hull, Georgia: Vietnam memorial on farm of John Snyder.

Snellville, Georgia: Snellville Vietnam Memorial.

Other Georgia Memorials

Atlanta: Flagpole and monument located on State Capitol grounds. Dedicated July 4, 1979.

Elberton: Memorial dedicated at high school to two students killed in Vietnam. Located on the football field. Dedicated October 1985.

Guam

Andersen Air Force Base

The Arc Light Memorial is dedicated to seventy-five men who lost their lives flying B-52 missions between January 1965 and December 1972 in Vietnam. It was dedicated February 12, 1974, at Andersen Air Force Base on Guam. The memorial consists of a B-52 known as "Old 100" for its tail number, 55-0100. The noble aircraft flew more than 5,000 hours in battle.

Andersen Air Force Base, Guam: The Arc Light Memorial.

71

Hawaii

Honolulu

The National Memorial Cemetery of the Pacific and the Honolulu Memorial are located in Puowaina Crater, an extinct volcano on Puowaina Drive in Honolulu. This site was chosen as one of two resting places in the Pacific area for the remains of World War II dead, the other site being in Manila. Eight hundred United States servicemen who died in Korea and Vietnam are also buried here.

The Court of Honor at the cemetery consists of a chapel, two map galleries, two flagpoles, and a pool of water. On the front of the chapel is a thirty-foot statue of a female figure holding a laurel branch and a quote from President Abraham Lincoln:

> The solemn pride that must be yours to have laid so costly a sacrifice upon the altar of freedom.

Descending from the chapel to the floor of the crater are the marble panels of the Courts of the Missing, engraved with the names of 28,778 Americans who were missing in action or lost or buried at sea during World War II, Korea, and Vietnam. The two courts containing names of 2,489 M.I.A.s from Vietnam were completed and dedicated in May of 1980.

There is also in Honolulu an eternal flame dedicated to all veterans.

Opposite: *Honolulu, Hawaii: The Court of Honor at the National Memorial Cemetery of the Pacific.*

Idaho

Idaho Falls

A small group of Vietnam veterans from the Upper Snake River Valley in Idaho dreamed of having a memorial in their area to honor all Idaho veterans of the war and especially those who died or are still missing in action. To carry out their dream, they helped establish the Idaho Freedom Bird State Vietnam Veterans Memorial Fund. A site in Freeman Park, in the city of Idaho Falls, was donated for the project. The sight overlooks the nearby Snake River.

Tom Criswell, a Vietnam veteran who served as a captain with the Army's 116th Engineering Battalion, designed the massive, twenty-four-foot-high memorial. The structure is an inverted "V" of polished stainless steel. The names of those lost or missing will be displayed on one leg of the "V." A relief sculpture depicting those who served will be on the other leg, along with a copper-etched map of Southeast Asia. The fund hopes to raise the $125,000 needed to build the monument in the near future.

Mountain Home Air Force Base

Mountain Home Air Force Base is the location of an F-111 memorial park. This park was dedicated Sept. 7, 1979. The focal point of the park is a windswept F-111 aircraft display with a touching monument plaque. The inscription on the plaque reads as follows:

> This park is dedicated to all those who participated in F-111 combat operations during the Southeast Asian conflict. Flying out of Takhli RTAFB, Thailand, the crews flew over 3,250 combat sorties beginning in

Mountain Home Air Force Base, Idaho: Mounted F-111 in memorial park.

1968, ranging from strikes over the highly defended capital of North Vietnam, to the harassment of Cambodian patrol boats during the Mayaquez incident of 1975. Nicknamed "Whispering Death" by the North Vietnamese, the F-111 missions were characterized by high speed, tree top level approaches into the heart of the enemy's country, virtually undetected by the defensive radar systems. The F-111's pinpoint accuracy during night operation, unparalleled in the history of airpower, gave the USAF the needed capability to keep "round the clock" pressure on the enemy. This display aircraft (no. 639776A) is on permanent loan from the USAF museum and is decorated with the names of the aircrew and the tail number of the first F-111 lost in combat on 28 March 1968.

We salute the following crew members who gave their lives for the preservation of freedom while flying the F-111 into the area of warfare:

28 March 1968
Col. Henry E. MacCann
Capt. Dennis L. Graham

22 April 1968
Lt. Comm. David L. Cooley (USN)
Col. Edwin D. Palmgren

28 September 1972
Col. William C. Coltman
Capt. Robert A. Brett, Jr.

17 October 1972
Major James A. Hockride
Capt. Allen U. Graham

7 November 1972
Lt. Col. Robert M. Brown
Lt. Col. Robert D. Morrissey

20 November 1972
Capt. Ronald D. Stafford
Capt. Charles J. Caffarelli

18 December 1972
Col. Robert J. Ward
Lt. Col. James R. McElvin

Dedicated 7 September 1979

Other Idaho Memorials

Boise: P.O.W./M.I.A. memorial located in Veterans State Park.

Illinois

Chicago

In recognition of his exceptional gallantry, the city of Chicago has named a 10½-acre park on Lake Michigan after P.F.C. Milton Lee Olive. This was perhaps the first Vietnam veterans memorial in America, as it was dedicated in the summer of 1966. The Congressional Medal of Honor was presented posthumously to P.F.C. Olive for his actions in the vicinity of Phu Cuong, Republic of Vietnam, on October 22, 1965. According to his citation, P.F.C. Olive, who served with the 503rd Infantry, 173rd Airborne Brigade, grabbed a Viet Cong grenade and fell on it in order to save the lives of four other soldiers.

The original stone of the monument was destroyed by vandals. A new eight-foot stone slab with large bronze plaque was rededicated by Mayor Richard J. Daley on July 3, 1970, with P.F.C. Olive's parents and other dignitaries present. The plaque bears the image of the young paratrooper and the complete text of his citation for bravery.

The park itself has a spectacular view of the Chicago skyline, beautiful landscaping, and five circular fountains which represent the five Great Lakes. The monument itself stands in the center of the park, which is visited by thousands of Chicago residents each week.

Joliet

"Joliet Junior College, the oldest public community college in the nation, may well be the first college campus where the seeds of conflict sown in the 1960's are laid to rest." So reads, in part, the invitation to the May 19, 1985, dedication of the Vietnam veterans memorial at the college. A

Chicago, Illinois: (Top) *Monument in memory of P.F.C. Milton Lee Olive. (Bottom) View of Chicago skyline from Milton Olive Memorial Park.*

Joliet, Illinois: Monument on the campus of Joliet Junior College is dedicated to the Vietnam veterans of America.

groundswell of support for the idea of such a tribute followed the suggestion made by Mark Johnson, a student trustee to the college's board of trustees.

The memorial includes both a permanent on-campus monument and a perpetual, living memorial in the form of an annual scholarship. The monument itself consists of engraved black granite panels built into the fireplace on "the Bridge," an enclosed section of concourse spanning the campus's lake. This is a focal point of campus activity.

Lake LaDonna

Lamont Gaston promised a dying young Marine in Vietnam that he would not forget him, and he didn't. When Lamont came home he built a Vietnam veterans memorial of his own in his recreational park at Lake LaDonna, near Oregon, Illinois. Pathways throughout the park are dedicated to the people who served in different areas of Vietnam. The park itself is a popular location for veterans' campouts, especially for the

Lake LaDonna, Illinois: Scenes from memorial park built by Lamont Gaston. Top: *Memorial monument in park.* Bottom: *Sign welcomes visitors to park.*

members of Vietnow, a large organization for which Mr. Gaston serves as national president. The stirring message on his monument reads:

> This park stands as a living tribute to the men who served their country during the Vietnam War. The whispering winds from the battlefields of Vietnam carrying the names of fathers, husbands, brothers, sons, and friends will perhaps someday fade. To those who returned the memories of their fallen brothers, the anguish of being neglected by their nation, and the hope for the future to bring an understanding of what happened over there, go on forever.

Mattoon

The Vietnam Veterans Cross is a symbol made from one upright and one inverted "V." The cross represents pride and sacrifice as well as the frustration experienced since the war. Jim and Bill Highland, both Vietnam vets, chose the emblem to adorn the Coles County Vietnam Veterans Memorial they designed.

The solemn black granite monument was built by the Mattoon, Illinois, V.F.W. Post 4325. It is located in Peterson Park in Mattoon.

Scott Air Force Base

The airmen of Scott Air Force Base in Illinois paid tribute to five of their own who made the supreme sacrifice in the war in Southeast Asia. Five concrete piers with bronze plaques mark streets that were renamed in January of 1979 to honor these heroes.

First Street was renamed King Street in memory of Chief Master Sergeant Charles D. King, who earned the Air Force Cross (posthumously) for extraordinary heroism as a pararescueman in recovering a downed U.S.A.F. pilot in Southeast Asia in December of 1968.

Second Street was renamed Pitsenbarger Street in memory of Airman First Class William H. Pitsenbarger, who earned the Air Force Cross (posthumously) for extraordinary heroism while administering medical treatment to wounded Americans while under heavy sniper and mortar fire in April of 1966. Airman Pitsenbarger was the first airman to receive the Air Force Cross, and the Air Force Sergeants Association presents an award for heroism to honor him each year.

Third Street was renamed in honor of Airman First Class Darryl G. Winters, who earned the Distinguished Flying Cross and the Air Medal (posthumously) for extraordinary achievement while participating in aerial flight as a motion picture camera technician in July of 1966. Airman Winters was participating in his 207th flight in an F-100 when the plane was downed by enemy gunfire.

Sixth Street was renamed Martin Street in honor of Capt. Duane W. Martin, who was killed as he attempted to escape as a Prisoner of War in July 1966. Capt. Martin's rescue helicopter had crashed in September of 1965 during an attempt to save a downed pilot. He was taken prisoner by the enemy at that time. Capt. Martin was awarded the Air Force Cross for extraordinary heroism, as well as the Purple Heart.

Mattoon, Illinois: Two sides of the Coles County Vietnam Veterans Memorial.

Eleventh Street was renamed in honor of Maj. Bernard L. Bucher, who was awarded the Air Force Cross (posthumously) for extraordinary heroism in May of 1968. Major Bucher attempted to land his C-130 aircraft on a primitive runway under heavy enemy fire to rescue friendly forces from Kham Duc airfield. His aircraft crashed and burned after takeoff. Maj. Bucher had also received nine other medals during his military career, which spanned three wars.

Also at the Scott Air Force Base: an AirLifters Memorial of black stone (dedicated June 28, 1979), and a P.O.W./M.I.A. memorial tree with bronze plaque (dedicated April 28, 1971).

Silvis

An unpaved, dusty little street, only a block and a half long, is believed to be the home of more American servicemen and more heroes who died in our nation's wars than any other area of its size in the entire country. Second Street in Silvis, Illinois, was renamed Hero Street U.S.A. in 1968, and rightly so. It is known that over ninety men, and now one woman, from this street served in the armed forces. Fifteen of them died while serving during wartime. Many were highly decorated heroes. Twelve died in World War II, two in Korea, and one in Vietnam. Eight of these were from the original Mexican-American families who settled in this area.

The proud, predominantly Mexican-American community has done much to recognize its heroes. Joseph Terronez, alderman to the area, served as chairman of the committee that developed the idea of Hero Street U.S.A., and later the Hero Street Memorial Park. The committee worked with architect Edward Angerer, project engineer Anthony Terronez, and the Axel Carlson Construction Company to erect the park, which was dedicated in 1971. The park itself is built into the side of a hill, known as Billy Goat Bluff.

At the top of the hill, there is a grotto where the names of the deceased are inscribed. At the bottom is a park area with playground equipment, a full basketball court, tire swings, and a concrete slide built into the hillside. Originally funds from the United States Department of Housing and Urban Development were used. The town has since received a $125,000 grant from the state of Illinois for renovation of the park.

This is indeed a unique memorial to a most remarkable all–American community.

Springfield

The location of the Illinois State Vietnam Veterans Memorial is the capital city of Springfield. Large walls of both black and gray granite encircle an eternal flame. On the walls are engraved the 2,946 names of all Illinois residents who gave their lives during the war in the name of freedom.

The dedication took place over the weekend of November 21–22, 1987. A 48-hour vigil at the memorial was held, along with a veterans parade. Mike Ferguson, of Springfield, headed a memorial committee comprised of veterans and citizens from around the state.

A part of the memorial inscription reads:

To those who died, honor and eternal rest
To those still in bondage, remembrance and hope
To those who returned, gratitude and peace

Streator

Vietnam veterans in Streator, Illinois, wanted to involve young people in their memorial project, in order to help answer some of the difficult questions that are often asked about the war. So a contest was held at the local high school art department for the best original design for the memorial.

The first place prize of a $50.00 savings bond went to a sophomore, Jeff Parker. He envisioned a three-part memorial in black concrete, with a plexiglass-protected, life-size painting of the statue of three soldiers that stands before "The Wall" in Washington, D.C.

The small group of seven Vietnam veterans then turned the design into reality through over 2,000 man-hours in fundraising efforts. They held dances, sold raffle tickets, and collected donations from citizens in order to pay for their own memorial. They were greatly encouraged by the amount of community support they received.

The dedication of the monument in City Park was held October 25, 1986. A crowd of over 1,000 stood in the pouring rain to listen to the dedication ceremony and watch the helicopter fly-over in tribute to area

Opposite: Springfield, Illinois: Drawing of the Illinois State Vietnam Veterans Memorial.

Streator, Illinois: The Streator Vietnam Veterans Memorial.

veterans who served and died in Vietnam. The striking memorial is in a
highly visible location and is considered to be a notable asset to the community. The city recently agreed to turn a parking lot in front of the
monument into a grass plaza, to enhance the beauty of this outstanding
tribute.

Other Illinois Memorials

Chicago: Fountain with flags, located in the center of the city.

Freeport: Proposed statue to be located on the Stephenson County Courthouse lawn.

Melvin: Names of ninety-four area men and women who served in Vietnam inscribed on two granite monoliths.

Ottawa: Veterans Memorial Bridge.

Potomac: Park dedicated to local resident killed in Vietnam.

Springfield: Veterans Parkway.

Sycamore: Plaque with names of nineteen men, located on courthouse lawn. Dedicated November 10, 1985.

Indiana

Evansville

The Downtown Civitan Club of Evansville, Indiana, presented the city with a monument honoring Vanderburgh County servicemen who were killed in Vietnam. The monument is located on the downtown walkway on Main Street. It was dedicated on January 29, 1973, and is one of the first memorials built following the withdrawal of American forces from Vietnam.

Evansville, Indiana–Henderson, Kentucky

Surely one of the largest Vietnam memorials in the country must be the Bi-State Vietnam Gold Star Memorial Bridge, which spans the Ohio River between Evansville, Indiana, and Henderson, Kentucky. Actually they are twin bridges, each carrying traffic one way between the two states. Through the efforts of a fraternity at the University of Evansville, the bridges were named and dedicated on May 31, 1969. The date makes this bridge one of the earliest memorials dedicated to those who gave everything in the war in Southeast Asia.

Grissom Air Force Base

Many Air Force bases have "Freedom Trees" planted in memory of Americans who served, died, and are still missing. One such tree and adjoining monument is at Grissom Air Force Base in Indiana. The following sentiment is expressed on this monument:

Top: *Evansville, Indiana: Monument honoring Vanderburgh County servicemen killed in Vietnam.* Bottom: *Evansville, Indiana–Henderson, Kentucky: These twin bridges spanning the Ohio River comprise the Bi-State Vietnam Gold Star Memorial Bridge.*

As this tree shall flourish and grow, so shall our hopes and prayers that peace will prevail on this earth forever.

Grissom Air Force Base, Indiana: The Freedom Tree and accompanying monument in memory of American servicemen.

Hebron

Three large boulders encircle the flagpole at Stoney Run Park, near Hebron, Indiana. On one of the boulders is a plaque dedicating the site to the men and women of Lake County who served and died in Vietnam. Surrounding the boulders are evergreen trees and shrubs, along with brick benches and walkways. This peaceful memorial was completed and dedicated in 1973.

Hobart

Was there a "doughboy" in Vietnam? No, but the spirit of the American soldier fighting to uphold the rights of others was just as prevalent in the jungles of Vietnam as in the First World War. That spirit is symbolized in the doughboy statue (World War I–vintage American soldier) atop the Veterans Monument in the center of Hobart, Indiana.

This monument is a source of pride to citizens of Hobart and is the scene of many ceremonies. The monument bears plaques honoring the veterans of the Vietnam War as well as veterans of other wars. After all, a veteran is a veteran is a veteran.

Laconia

The "Three Steps of Hell" is the name of the memorial Lloyd H. Krohn built himself on his farm in Laconia, Indiana. The six-foot-high brick monument was constructed in a three-tier effect representing Command Sgt. Maj. Krohn's feelings on Vietnam:

Step 1 – Why in hell did we get involved in the first place?
Step 2 – We fought like hell while we were there. ˙
Step 3 – Most of us were lucky as hell to get out of there when we did.

Twenty-six years in the Army, with a combined thirty-two months of service with Armored Cavalry Regiments in Vietnam, gives Krohn the knowledge, authority, and right to name his monument in this manner. He began building his monument on a cold winter's day in December of 1982 so that it would be ready for a Memorial Day dedication in 1983. Since the dedication, the monument has been kept open year-round for visitors from all over the country.

Hebron, Indiana: Vietnam Veterans Memorial at Stoney Run Park has a commemorative plaque (top) *in the center of an evergreen garden* (bottom).

Top: *Hobart, Indiana: Hobart Veterans Monument with "Doughboy" statue commemorating all American soldiers.* Bottom: *Laconia, Illinois: Lloyd H. Krohn's "Three Steps of Hell" Vietnam memorial.*

Other Indiana Memorials

Booneville: Solid aluminum monument with plaque. Located on Courthouse Square. Dedicated in 1982.

Brookville: Four-sided stone wall with plaques honoring veterans of all wars. Located at Franklin County Seat grounds. Dedicated November 11, 1983.

Fort Wayne: War Veterans Memorial Shrine. A chapel and museum dedicated to all war veterans. Located on O'Day Road.

Indianapolis: The Indiana War Memorial dedicated to all veterans. Located between Meridian and Pennsylvania streets.

Kokomo: Monument with plaques listing names of those who served and those who died from Howard County. Located in the City Courthouse. Dedicated November 11, 1982.

Noblesville: Monument with plaque with seventeen area men killed in Vietnam. Located on Hamilton County Courthouse grounds. Dedicated 1971.

Princeton: Proposed monument to be built at Courthouse.

Other memorials are located in East Chicago and Richmond.

Iowa

Council Bluffs

Two fathers led the effort in their community to establish a memorial to area veterans who had fought and died in Vietnam. Ross Grego's twenty-year old son, Marine Private Phillip Grego, was killed in Vietnam on August 23, 1966. Verlow King also has a son who is a Vietnam veteran.

The two men worked to raise $21,000 to erect the memorial in Bayliss

Council Bluffs, Iowa: Two sides of the Pottawattamie County Vietnam Veterans Memorial.

95

Park, which is located in Council Bluffs, Iowa. The memorial lists the names of thirty-nine Pottawattamie County residents who died or are listed as missing in action. The seven-ton granite tribute was dedicated September 29, 1984, with a National Guard firing squad and a color guard made up of Navy, Air Force, Army, and Marine representatives.

The next phase of this project will be to add a six-foot bronze statue of an infantryman to the top of the memorial, along with three granite benches beside it. The statue will appear to gaze down on viewers as they read the names listed. Omaha sculptor John Lajba was chosen to prepare the statue of a young Vietnam-era Marine.

Des Moines

"A Reflection of Hope" is the title of the Iowa Vietnam Veterans Memorial near the Capitol building in Des Moines. It was dedicated before a crowd of hundreds on May 28, 1984. The beautiful curved wall is made of the same polished black granite found in the National Vietnam Veterans Memorial in Washington, D.C.

The movement to build a monument in Iowa was led by Mrs. Jacqueline Day, mother of a wounded Vietnam veteran and a staunch, hardworking advocate for all Vietnam veterans. Mrs. Day twice visited troops in Vietnam, once in 1967 and again in 1970. She has volunteered for several years at the V.A. Medical Center in Des Moines. She was devoted to the task of raising the funds needed to make Iowa's Vietnam Veterans Monument so special.

The final design chosen was a combination of two entries to a statewide contest. Tim Salisbury of Newton and Mary Jane Fisher of Des Moines both contributed to the design. Across the top of the monument, above the names of 855 Iowans lost in Vietnam, are these simple words:

A Reflection of Hope

A monument established by the citizens of Iowa to honor Iowans who served during the Vietnam War. These absent friends will never be forgotten.

Also in Des Moines, the new flagpole at Stew Hanson's Dodge City, Inc., holds what is believed to be the largest American flag to fly between Chicago and Denver. It measures 30 by 50 feet. The flagpole was dedicated to Vietnam veterans on November 28, 1987. Mr. Hanson's son, Dennis, is

Des Moines, Iowa: Two views of the Iowa Vietnam Veterans Memorial, entitled "A Reflection of Hope."

a Vietnam veteran, as are several of his employees. This tribute was erected to honor their service to their country.

Sac County

Veterans Park on U.S. Highway 20, in Sac County, Iowa, is the sight of a monument for all Vietnam veterans from that area. The granite stone

Top: *Des Moines, Iowa: Flagpole at Stew Hanson's Dodge City is dedicated to Vietnam veterans.* Bottom: *Sac County, Iowa: Two sides of the Sac County Vietnam Veterans Memorial.*

Waterloo, Iowa: Two views of the Blackhawk County Vietnam Veterans Memorial.

was erected by the Sac County American Legion. It has a bronze plaque on its reverse side naming seven county residents who were killed in the war. The monument was dedicated during Memorial Day ceremonies in 1984.

Waterloo

On the east side of the Cedar River, in downtown Waterloo, Iowa, stands a tall, polished, black granite monument to the Vietnam veterans of Blackhawk County. The monument, designed by R.J. Lundgren, was dedicated on Veterans Day of 1986. Danny Hanson of Cedar Falls initiated the project and worked with a local railroad company to raise the needed funds.

Other Iowa Memorials

Des Moines: Flagpole and plaques dedicated to Vietnam veterans. Located in front of the Federal Building.

Lineville: Gosh-Moore Park. Dedicated to two local men killed in Vietnam.

Scotts Ridge: Park located at Scotts Ridge Church. Dedicated to local veterans who died in the war. Located on Highway 65-69, south of Des Moines.

Winterset: Stone monument with bronze plaque listing names of county men killed in the war.

Other memorials are located in Dubuque, Elkater, and Manchester.

Kansas

McConnell Air Force Base

A living tribute in Kansas is the Memorial Walk at McConnell Air Force Base, which was dedicated May 16, 1976. This is a lovely, tree-lined asphalt pathway extending from the east gate, along Kansas Avenue, to the chapel. Each tree along the walk has a natural stone marker with a bronze plaque engraved with the name of a serviceperson from McConnell who gave his or her life while serving in Southeast Asia or on duty at McConnell during or after the war. As of 1980, 51 trees had been planted, 27 of which honor F-105 pilots and maintenance personnel.

Also included in McConnell's tribute is a proud F-105 permanently mounted beside a bronze marker which reads simply, "For those who have flown and died."

McConnell Air Force Base, Kansas: Mounted F-105, part of McConnell's Memorial Walk.

Wichita

Headquartered in Wichita, the Red River Valley Fighter Pilots Association (the River Rats) maintains a living memorial in the form of a scholarship fund for the sons and daughters of those who were killed in action or are still missing in action in Southeast Asia. In 1985 they will offer over a quarter of a million dollars in grants to hundreds of these deserving students. This fine organization is composed of American servicemen who flew in the Red River Valley of North Vietnam, said to be the most heavily defended airspace in the history of aerial warfare.

Kentucky

Owensboro

The city of Owensboro, Kentucky, has joined its tributes to local veterans together at the site of the Sports Center Complex. The city moved the Korean and Vietnam Veterans Memorial, built in 1974, from Chautauqua Park to its new location adjacent to the World War II Monument, built in 1947. Further improvements to the joint memorial were later made.

Other Kentucky Memorials

Bardstown: Two concrete memorials located near the Nelson County Courthouse listing fourteen local residents killed in action in Vietnam.

Frankfort: Proposed monument.

Hawesville: Three stone markers from all wars, located on the Courthouse lawn.

Louisville: Proposed monument of a giant sundial. A shadow will fall on each name listed on the day that the person died. A computer was used to compile the data necessary to accomplish this feat.

Owensboro, Kentucky: Owensboro Korean and Vietnam Veterans Memorial was moved to a location adjacent to Owensboro World War II monument.

Louisiana

New Orleans

Eight hundred eighty-one citizens of Louisiana lost their lives in Vietnam. Their sacrifices are forever memorialized in the bronze figures of three weary young soldiers as they carry a wounded comrade up a hillside to safety.

This inspiring monument, designed by Vietnam veteran Milton Pounds, is located on the Plaza Level of the Superdome in New Orleans. It was sculpted by William Ludwig, using the ancient "lost wax" process,

New Orleans, Louisiana: Louisiana Vietnam Veterans Memorial, located on the Plaza Level of the Superdome.

105

Ouachita Parish, Louisiana: Two sides of the Ouachita Parish Memorial. Shown left to right in bottom photo are Michael K. Hooks, Loyde Arender, and Sylvester Smith, Jr., who collected money for the memorial.

which results in remarkably realistic detail. Official military uniforms, weapons, and equipment were used by live models in order to recreate the scene for the sculptor.

The Louisiana Vietnam Veterans Memorial Fund, a program of the Louisiana Vietnam Veterans Leadership Program, was responsible for raising the needed funds from private contributions. The memorial honoring the more than 150,000 Louisiana residents who served their country during the Vietnam era was dedicated in ceremonies held on Veterans Day, November 11, 1984.

Ouachita Parish

The polished white granite of the Ouachita Parish Memorial reflected the reverent faces of a crowd of nearly 200 gathered before it that November day in 1984. People who had come to help dedicate the beautiful monument searched for the names of their sons, brothers, fathers, or friends who did not come home from the war. The monument in Monroe bears the names of forty men from Ouachita Parish who died in combat.

Loyde P. Arender envisioned a monument to his fellow Vietnam veterans and designed it with four military crests, the Purple Heart, and an honor roll of names on one side and an eagle and the dragon design from the Vietnam service medal on the reverse side. In his letter to the authors, Loyde wrote:

> I served in Vietnam from December 1968 until March 1970. I served as a machine gunner in the infantry with Kilo Company, 3rd Battalion, 26th Marines. When I left Vietnam, I came home with "an appreciation for life" that will remain with me always. It may be a cliche, but "For Those Who Fight for it, Life has a Meaning that the Protected will never know."
>
> This appreciation for life and the fact that I am an American who loves the Lord and his fellow man, has inspired me to work with other Vietnam veterans. I designed the Ouachita Parish Memorial in such a way as to honor Both, the men who served and the men who were killed in Vietnam. To live on in the hearts of others is to never die.

Maine

Augusta

Two important things happen when a community works together to erect a monument to its Vietnam veterans. First, an avenue is finally opened to the public to express the respect and honor that they have felt for those amongst them who answered their country's call under the most difficult of circumstances. Secondly, the veterans themselves are able to say, "Yes, I was there"; to receive the recognition and gratitude of their peers that went unsaid for so many years; and to pay homage to the people they served with during the war.

Both happenings were especially apparent in the recent construction of the Maine Vietnam Veterans Memorial in Augusta. Phil Vampatella, executive director of the Vietnam Veterans Leadership Program of Maine, Inc., had this to say about the response to his group's project:

> . . . we have seen an incredible outpouring of warmth and recognition from virtually the entire State of Maine. Cooperation and encouragement from government, the news media, private industry, the public sector, and most of all, from thousands of individuals throughout the state, including veterans from all wars, have made this Memorial project one of the most significant to ever benefit Maine's Vietnam veterans.

The October 19, 1985, dedication of the memorial drew a crowd of nearly 2,000. Many of these were Vietnam veterans, coming together at last to be honored by their state. They banded together in pairs and in groups to share the memories evoked by the massive tribute. Several were proud to wear again the uniforms representing their service.

Vietnam vets themselves played a major role in the actual construction of this truly one-of-a-kind memorial. Besides the members of the V.V.L.P.

Augusta, Maine: The Maine Vietnam Veterans Memorial.

of Maine, there were steelworkers who volunteered their time to carve out the outline of the three soldiers in the first steel triangle; truck drivers who transported the finished pieces to the site near the State House; a state trooper who escorted the trucks along their way; and scores of others who contributed in their own ways.

The striking monument, designed by Roger Richmond, consists mainly of two triangles: the first a huge three-quarter-inch Corten steel plate, cut with the image of two soldiers helping a wounded comrade, and another, taller plate which stands behind the first and acts to reflect the outlined image of the soldiers.

Benton

Family and friends of Sgt. Brian L. Buker raised funds to erect a granite monument on the front lawn of the small church in Benton that he attended

SGT. BRIAN L. BUKER MEMORIAL

SGT BRIAN L. BUKER WAS KILLED IN ACTION
WHILE SERVING WITH AN ARMY SPECIAL FORCES UNIT
IN VIETNAM, ON APRIL 5TH 1970
HE WAS POSTHUMOUSLY AWARDED
OUR NATIONS HIGHEST DECORATION
THE CONGRESSIONAL MEDAL OF HONOR
FOR BRAVERY UNDER FIRE, ABOVE AND BEYOND
THE CALL OF DUTY

HE WILL LIVE IN OUR HEARTS FOREVER

OTHERS KILLED IN ACTION
WORLD WAR II
KENNETH E. NORTON D.O.W. ARMY NOV. 1 1943
ROBERT J. GIBBS K.I.A. NAVY AIR FORCE APR 18 1944
EVERSON C. LOVEJOY K.I.A. ARMY DEC 17 1944
RAYMOND C. TAYLOR IN I.A NAVY DEC 10 1944
WORLD WAR I
HERBERT W. DAVIS D.O.W. ARMY SEPT 22 1918
OTHERS WHO DIED IN SERVICE
GEORGE A. PHILBROOK D.O.R.D. ARMY 1918
JAMES POTTLE JR. D.O.R.D. AIR FORCE APR 20 1970

ERECTED BY FAMILIES, FRIENDS AND TOWN SPEOPLE

Top: *Benton, Maine: A monument to the memory of Brian L. Buker, who died in Vietnam, stands in front of this Benton church.* Bottom: *Benton, Maine: The Brian L. Buker Memorial.*

as a child. The monument honors Brian and several other area war veterans, whose names are also engraved thereon.

Below the likeness of Brian's smiling face on the stone is etched the Congressional Medal of Honor awarded to him for his gallantry, and these words:

> Sgt. Brian L. Buker was killed in action while serving with an Army Special Forces unit in Vietnam, on April 5, 1970. He was posthumously awarded our nation's highest decoration, the Congressional Medal of Honor, for bravery under fire, above and beyond the call of duty.
>
> He will live in our hearts forever.

Other Maine Memorials

South Berwick: Granite marker with bronze plaque.

Maryland

U.S. Naval Academy at Annapolis: Bronze plaque on a granite slab. Located in Academy Cemetery. Dedicated May of 1975.
Baltimore: Proposed monument at Federal Hill.

Massachusetts

Danvers

A four-sided granite pillar honoring veterans of World Wars I and II, Korea, and Vietnam now stands in front of the Town Hall in Danvers, Massachusetts, thanks to Vietnam veteran Robert MacDonald. Robert worked for over a year to solicit the $5,000 needed from local merchants.

Above the names of the five men lost in Vietnam are the three words so often uttered by veterans when remembering their fallen friends: "He's My Brother."

The somber sounds of a bugler playing taps, rifles sounding their salute, and a bagpipe's wail ended the June 9, 1984, dedication of this monument.

Danvers, Massachusetts: Memorial to veterans of World War I, World War II, Korea, and Vietnam.

Lynn, Massachusetts: Lynn Vietnam Veterans Memorial.

Lynn

The image of a young soldier, leaning forward with both hands on the helmet and rifle of his fallen friend, reminds citizens of Lynn, Massachusetts, of their thirty-three young neighbors who died in Vietnam. The long overdue remembrance in the City Hall Square was dedicated March 26, 1983, following a parade of over 1,000 Vietnam veterans from around the state. The Vietnam Veterans Memorial Committee, chaired by

Kevin Roach, worked diligently to inspire the community to come together to raise such a fitting tribute.

Newton

In 1970, Corporal Richard A. Likely of Newton, Massachusetts, wrote a letter to the editor of his hometown paper, the *Newton Graphic*. This is a part of that letter:

> I am writing this letter to tell people how Vietnam is in the eyes of a soldier over here.
> First I would like to say that Vietnam is an experience you have to go through to understand. No one can write to you their feelings of happiness at a job well done, or fear during a firefight, or sorrow when your best buddy gets killed. You have to be there to know what it is like.
> Vietnam is a beautiful country. The hills are so green. When it is not raining, the sky is so blue, birds fluttering all around and flowers of every color growing wild. The children are a world in themselves. . . .
> . . . Sometimes it's hard to remember there is a war going on, but you see war's battered faces everywhere: burned out villages, blown up bridges, bodies lifeless as coal. Still you push on, and when it's all over, you're glad you were there. . . .
> Vietnam is something different to everyone, but this is how it is to me — one lonely soldier fighting for peace.

On the morning of April 27, 1971, Corporal Likely was killed while on patrol near Chu Lai. In memory of him and twenty-two other Newton residents who died in the war, a monument was dedicated on Memorial Day, 1985. Four bridges nearby were also dedicated to Vietnam K.I.A.s, including Corporal Likely.

Peabody

"Unity"
"All We Have Is Each Other"

These inspiring words mark the base of a unique tri-monument in front of the City Hall in Peabody, Massachusetts. Three white granite slabs bear the names of ninety Peabody residents who died during World War II, the Korean War, and the Vietnam War. The monument was the result of a joint community effort to honor the veterans of these wars. The May 19, 1984, dedication ceremony attracted over 500 persons, including many Gold Star

Top: *Newton, Massachusetts: Newton Vietnam Era Veterans Memorial.* Bottom: *Peabody, Massachusetts: Memorial honoring veterans of World War II, Korea, and Vietnam.*

families, Medal of Honor recipients, service organizations, police and fire delegations, color guards, and a high school band. The ceremony began with a veterans march, which was especially meaningful to those who had never been awarded that honor by their hometown.

At the bottom of each slab are words from each war. They are:

World War II, "Glory Weeps the Brave"
Korean War, "The Line We Couldn't Cross"
Vietnam War, "We Trusted..."

Top: *Salem, Massachusetts: Memorial honoring veterans of World War II, Korea, and Vietnam.* Bottom: *Stoneham, Massachusetts: Vietnam Veterans Memorial.*

Salem

Near such historical landmarks as the House of the Seven Gables and the Witch House in Salem, Massachusetts, there stands a solemn monument to veterans who made the ultimate sacrifice in World War I, World

War II, Korea, and Vietnam. The memorial rests on the Salem Commons.

Springfield

The Springfield, Massachusetts, Vietnam Veterans Memorial speaks of the courage and sacrifice of Americans who served during the war. It was the concept of the Winchester Square Vietnam Era Veterans, Ltd., and the city of Springfield. The city financed the $5,000 cost of the monument, which is located in the downtown area, across from City Hall.

Three slate stones form a circle and represent an open book. Both sides of each slate are engraved with names of deceased or missing service people and the combat artwork of Vietnam veteran Bob L. Daniels.

A Vietnam veterans parade preceded the unveiling ceremonies in March of 1983.

Stoneham

Names of living and deceased veterans are both listed on the white granite Vietnam Veterans Memorial in Stoneham, Massachusetts. There are thirteen names of those who died in service during the era, and 260 names of those who served in Vietnam, including one female, Donna (Milio) Chaloux.

The memorial committee, led by chairperson Richard Del Rossi, sold buttons and bumper stickers and held two dances to raise funds for the tribute. Over 100 people also made personal contributions to the fund. The town of Stoneham donated $5,000 to the project.

The monument, which is located in front of the Town Hall, was dedicated November 4, 1984, with over 300 people in attendance. The epitaph on the monument reads, "They will be forever young, they gave us their tomorrows." These were words from the military funeral mass of Lt. Joseph T. Campbell, spoken by Monsignor John Sexton in June of 1968.

Other Massachusetts Memorials

Dorchester: Monument with names of those who died.

Westborough: Park renamed to Vietnam Veterans Park, with a monument.

Wrentham: Plaque.
Other memorials are located in these cities:
Beverly
Brookline
Chicopee
Fitchburg
Halliston
Hull
Hyannis
Nahant
Natick
Pembroke
Revere
South Boston
West Roxbury

Michigan

Coopersville

Originally dedicated to those who died in the World Wars, a monument in Coopersville, Michigan (Polkton Township), was updated with bronze plaques honoring those lost in Korea and Vietnam. The names of those who died or are still missing in all the wars are listed on the honor rolls.

Coopersville, Michigan: Monument honoring those lost in the World Wars, Korea, and Vietnam.

Detroit

The United States Coast Guard has served in every national war, including Vietnam. At the Coast Guard Air Station, Selfridge Air National Guard Base, in Detroit, there is a memorial dedicated to a young officer who died in that war.

Lieutenant Jack C. Rittichier was killed in action while flying as an exchange helicopter pilot with the United States Air Force in Vietnam. An aircraft hanger at the Selfridge Air National Guard Base is named after him. The memorial plaque reads:

Rittichier
Memorial
Hanger
In memory of
Lt. Jack C. Rittichier
Killed in Action
Republic of Vietnam
9 June 1968

In service to his nation
and
his fellow man

Fruitport

Fruitport, Michigan, is the site of two monuments for Vietnam veterans. One is the veterans monument near the General Offices, for all veterans. It was dedicated by the Bicentennial Committee in 1977. The other is the Vietnam Honor Roll, erected by V.F.W. Post 7803. This monument was dedicated in 1980 and has a sundial on the top.

Grand Rapids

Veterans Memorial Park in Grand Rapids is the sight of twin monuments to Vietnam veterans. Erected by citizens of Kent County, the monuments list the names of all county residents who died or are missing in the war. The monument on the left contains the names from A through K in the alphabetic listing, and the monument on the right has names from L through Z. They were dedicated in 1974.

Top: *Kentwood, Michigan: Three flagstaffs surround Vietnam memorial in Veterans Memorial Park.* Bottom: *Muskegon, Michigan: Vietnam Honor Roll at Veterans Memorial Park, located on an island.*

Opposite, left: Fruitport, Michigan: *Monument to all veterans of foreign wars.* Opposite, center: Fruitport, Michigan: *Vietnam Honor Roll.* Opposite, right: *Grand Rapids, Michigan: One of the matching pair of monuments to Vietnam veterans.*

Kentwood

The Vietnam veterans memorial in Kentwood, Michigan, is flanked by three tall flagstaffs. It is located in Veterans Memorial Park. The dedication took place in 1986.

Muskegon

Veterans Memorial Park is located on an island in Muskegon, Michigan. The Honor Roll for the Muskegon County veterans who lost their lives in Vietnam is located in the park.

Other Michigan Memorials

Grand Haven: Monument of granite with eternal flame.

Kalamazoo: Two memorials.

Lansing: Tall stone veterans monument topped with an eagle, flanked by smaller stones on either side. Located on State Capitol grounds. Dedicated November 11, 1982.

Monroe: "M"-shaped monument with granite walls.

Minnesota

Cushing

Geoffrey T. Steiner is a Vietnam veteran who cares. He shows his caring by planting trees — over 30,000 of them now — on his 100 acres of wilderness near Cushing, Minnesota, about 120 miles north of Minneapolis. His goal is to plant over 60,000 trees, approximately one for each person who died in Vietnam, as well as those still missing. Geof started planting in 1980, paying for the first trees by himself. Now most of the trees are donated to him by the state forestry department.

On Memorial Day, 1985, the Living Memorial Forest was formally dedicated. It is now recognized as an official memorial to Minnesota's Vietnam veterans. On Memorial Day, 1986, a granite memorial was dedicated. Inscribed on the stone is Proverbs 24:11–12 (Living Bible), which reads:

> Rescue those who are unjustly sentenced to death. Don't stand back and let them die. Don't try to disclaim responsibility by saying you don't know about it. For God who knows all hearts, knows yours, and He knows you knew! And He will reward everyone according to his deeds.

The stone symbolically rests beneath a large flagstaff from which fly the P.O.W./M.I.A. and American flags.

Geof was recognized nationally for his efforts by *People Weekly*, as one of their "Heroes of the Year" for 1986, in the "End of the Year Special Issue." He is active in the local Vietnam Veterans of America, Chapter 214, and serves as the state's V.V.A. chaplain.

But Geof is not willing to stop with the magnificent forest he is planting. He now envisions a counseling and education center for Vietnam veterans and their families, a combination P.O.W./M.I.A. National Mu-

St. Paul, Minnesota: "Monument to the Living" is dedicated to the survivors of all wars.

seum and "R. & R." healing center. He is actively recruiting volunteers to help him raise the needed funds for this latest monumental venture. This idea came from his great desire to help Vietnam veterans who are in need of emotional support, as well as to give the public information about the P.O.W.s and M.I.A.s who still wait in Southeast Asia. He is a man who cares deeply about his brothers and sisters who served with him in the jungles of Vietnam.

St. Paul

"A Monument to the Living" is a twelve-foot-high, welded steel tribute to the survivors of all wars. Rodger M. Brodin of Minneapolis created this statue, which is located near the Veterans Service Building in St. Paul, Minnesota. Mr. Brodin is also the sculptor who designed the national Vietnam Womens' Monument to be erected in Washington, D.C., near "The Wall."

This outstanding work of art is one of the few memorials dedicated to the survivors.

Other Minnesota Memorials

Paynesville: Veterans Memorial Park, with flagpole and boulder with plaque. Dedicated to all who served. Located on Lake Koronis. Dedicated November 11, 1976.

Mississippi

Keesler Air Force Base

The Mississippi Gulf Coast Chapter of the American Ex–Prisoners of War dedicated a marble monument to all American veterans on May 24, 1984. The marble slab sits atop a three-foot-high concrete block and bears the logo of the organization. It is located in front of Building 2816 on Gen. Daniel James Avenue, Keesler Air Force Base, Mississippi.

Other Mississippi Memorials

Jackson: Proposed memorial.

Keesler Air Force Base, Mississippi: Monument dedicated to all American veterans.

Missouri

Corder

Doug Lorenz and other members of V.F.W. Post 4288 and the post auxiliary worked together to raise funds for their black granite monument to veterans of all four wars. Funding came from many sources in the community, including families who had lost members in the wars. The Baker Memorial Company in Lexington, Missouri, was very cooperative in helping to produce the monument at their cost. Dedicated on May 25, 1987, the memorial is located at the V.F.W. Post, which is just outside Corder, Missouri.

Corder, Missouri: Monument to veterans of World War I, World War II, Korea and Vietnam.

Kansas City, Missouri: Two views of the multi-level fountain honoring Vietnam veterans.

Kansas City

To fit with their "City of Fountains" image, the Kansas City Vietnam Veterans Memorial Fund committee has chosen a multi-level fountain to honor the men and women from the surrounding areas who served in Southeast Asia. The fountain is entwined with a pathway that visitors may walk along as they reflect upon their memories of the war. More than 540 names, along with the image of the Purple Heart and the Vietnam Service Medal, are engraved in the granite walls behind the fountain.

Macon, Missouri: Memorial to those lost in Korea and Vietnam.

Macon

Another combined Korea and Vietnam memorial marker was unveiled at the 1985 Memorial Day services held at the Macon County Courthouse in Macon, Missouri. Representatives of American Legion Post 29, the Anne Helm Chapter of the D.A.R., Veterans of World War I, the V.F.W., Girl Scouts, Boy Scouts, and the Committee to Recognize Our Servicemen's Sacrifices (C.R.O.S.S.) were all present to remember area veterans in word, music, and prayer. This widely varied group showed that respect for American veterans has no age restrictions, as young and old alike shared in the reverence of the day.

Mountain Grove

The members of V.F.W. Post 3770 of Mountain Grove, Missouri, were very proud to dedicate their three-sided monument on May 27, 1985. It is

Mountain Grove, Missouri: Three-sided memorial pays tribute to area veterans of World War II, Korea, and Vietnam.

the first memorial in the town for the veterans of World War II, Korea, and Vietnam. Each of the three sides lists the names of those lost in one war. The dedication ceremony was complete with a twenty-one-gun salute and the playing of taps, which followed the reading of all the names on the memorial. This memorial is a unique way to honor the veterans of all three of our nation's last wars.

Other Missouri Memorials

Hartville: Stone monument with plaque listing names of Wright County residents killed in action. Located at the Courthouse.

Hillsboro: Plaque listing names of area residents killed in action.

Jefferson City: Ten-foot red granite obelisk with bronze eagle on top. Granite dedication plaque from Cole County. Also, gray brick wall with plaque listing names of those killed in action. Located in city government complex. Dedicated July 4, 1983.

Mansfield: Stone monument listing names of those killed in the war. Located in the Town Square. Dedicated in 1976.

St. Louis: Monument listing names of those killed in action.

Montana

Missoula

The city of Missoula, Montana, has plans to erect a memorial to all its Vietnam veterans in the near future. The proposed memorial will include a magnificent eight-foot sculpture of an angel carrying a wounded soldier. The wings of the angel will gently enfold the fallen American. This promises to be a truly unusual and beautiful memorial to Montana veterans.

Other Montana Memorials

Billings: A wall at the Vet Center with names of all the people from the state who were lost in the war.

Nebraska

Falls City

On the southeast corner of the Courthouse Square in Falls City, Nebraska, stands a tall granite monument to the veterans of World War II, Korea, and Vietnam. It was dedicated on July 28, 1984. The names of those from Richardson County who lost their lives during the wars are inscribed on three separate stones, one for each war.

Kearney

The Jaycees of Kearney, Nebraska, began a project to pay tribute to area Vietnam veterans in March of 1985. On May 26, 1986, they dedicated their monument, a podium-shaped, 5,000-pound slab of ebony mist granite. The attached plaque reads:

> A tribute in honor and memoriam: To those who served during the Vietnam War, 1964–75. Those who came back and those who did not. May Got grant love, understanding, and peace. From the Kearney Jaycees and the people of Nebraska.

At the dedication for the monument, which is located in Apollo Park, Nebraska, Governor Robert Kerrey, a Congressional Medal of Honor recipient for gallantry in Vietnam, was the guest speaker. A ten-day display of the half-size replica of the National Vietnam Veterans Memorial in Washington, D.C., was also part of the dedication in the park.

Falls City, Nebraska: Richardson County Memorial to veterans of World War II, Korea, and Vietnam.

Nebraska City

Flag Day, June 14, 1987, was the dedication date for the new Otoe County War Memorial in Nebraska City, Nebraska. It is located on the front lawn of the Otoe County Courthouse. The memorial consists of four marble tabloids engraved with the names of citizens who died during the last four of our nation's wars. A flag, dedication marker, and two granite benches complete the tribute.

Top: *Kearney, Nebraska: Vietnam veterans memorial in Apollo Park.* Bottom: *Nebraska City, Nebraska: Otoe County War Memorial.*

Other Nebraska Memorials

Bassett: Display case with photos dedicated to James Fletcher, Vietnam veteran. Located at American Legion.

Clay Center: Athletic field dedicated to a World War II veteran and a Vietnam veteran.

Norfolk: Memorial to Korean and Vietnam veterans. Located in Prospect Hill Cemetery.

Schuyler: Marble monument with eternal flame and iron fencing. Located on the Courthouse lawn.

Weeping Water: Flagpole dedicated to Captain Donovan Walters. Located at Enchanted Trails.

West Point: Monument dedicated to John Bring, Vietnam veteran. Located on the Courthouse lawn.

Nevada

Nellis Air Force Base

The main entrance of the Tactical Fighter Weapons Center at Nellis Air Force Base houses a unique tribute to American P.O.W.s and M.I.A.s still held in Southeast Asia. It consists of a Keith Ferris lithograph entitled "Forget Me Not," a Freedom Bell, and a pair of Son Tay sneakers. The bell, which was not rung until August 25, 1973, upon the release of some of our P.O.W.s, was the idea of the 388th Tactical Fighter Wing stationed in Thailand in 1967. The sneakers were also untied for that occasion. Mr. Ferris's original painting is displayed in the office of the chairman of the Joint Chiefs of Staff at the Pentagon.

Reno

An eight-foot-high torch stands beside a bronze plaque in downtown Reno, Nevada, at the corner of Virginia and State streets. It is the Vietnam Veteran's Memorial Flame. The inscription on the plaque reads:

> Freedom Flame, dedicated March 24, 1973 by Major Robert F. Waggoner, USAF, former P.O.W., in honor of all Vietnam Veterans.

Other Nevada Memorials

Las Vegas: Marker with names engraved.

New Hampshire

Derry

On July 4, 1983, the town of Derry, New Hampshire, dedicated a memorial to veterans of both the Korean and Vietnam wars. Many people attended the ceremony. Speakers included Governor Sununu, Senator Gordon Humphrey, Representative Norman D'Amours, House minority leader Chris Spirou, and State Veterans Council director David W. Houle.

Manchester

Citizens of Manchester, New Hampshire, celebrated Veterans Day, 1985, by dedicating the new Veterans Memorial Park, formerly Merrimack Common, in the center of the city. A huge, 135-foot flagstaff there is surrounded by four black granite blocks honoring veterans of World War I, World War II, Korea, and Vietnam. The nearby Civil War memorial fountain was refurbished for the occasion. The Greater Manchester Veterans Council appointed past commander Mike Lopez to be in charge of the special events, which included dedication ceremonies and the annual Veterans Day parade.

Also in Manchester, dedication of the Vietnam Veterans Memorial Bridge on I-89 between Vermont and New Hampshire took place October 15, 1983, as part of the Vietnam Veterans Homecoming Weekend in New Hampshire. The speakers at the dedication of the bridge included Governor Sununu, Representative Chris Spirou and State Veterans Council director David W. Houle. Also included in the weekend's events were opening

Troy, New Hampshire: Town memorial to veterans of World War II, Korea, and Vietnam.

ceremonies by the governor and presentation to the governor of the New Hampshire Vietnam Veteran Commemorative Medal, designed by Keith Fleury and engraved by Dick Herget. The governor later presented a state flag to the New Hampshire Vietnam Veteran Vigil Delegation, which will fly the flag near "The Wall" in Washington, D.C. On the last day of the weekend, October 16, 1983, there was a reading of the names of New Hampshire's 221 casualties from the Vietnam War. At the ending of the reading David Houle quoted the words of John Donne, "Never send to know for whom the bell tolls; it tolls for thee." With these words, church bells throughout the state of New Hampshire rang to honor the veterans.

Troy

The small mill town of Troy, New Hampshire, was settled in the 1700s and incorporated in 1815. Since its beginnings, Troy has been represented in every war and conflict from the early years of America's history. On the Common in Troy there have long been two tributes to veterans: the World

War I and the Civil War monuments. On November 17, 1985, a third monument was added to honor all veterans of World War II, Korea, and Vietnam.

In 1983 the Town Warrant authorized the formation of a committee of six members to develop plans for a new veterans monument. The American Legion Post 56 and V.F.W. Post 10289 were represented on the committee. In 1985 the committee asked for and was granted $13,000 from the town to aid in constructing the monument they had chosen.

The monument attests to the pride the town of Troy has in its citizens' service to their nation and the contributions these veterans made to their community when they returned home.

Other New Hampshire Memorials

Rindge: The Cathedral of the Pines. Located on a mountain ridge. There is a memorial to all servicewomen, as well as a building which houses memorabilia from many wars.

Jaffrey: Monument located on the river bank in the center of town.

New Jersey

McGuire Air Force Base: (1) Freedom Tree dedicated to all M.I.A./P.O.W.s. Located in front of the Welcome Center. Dedicated in 1973. (2) C-123 aircraft dedicated as a tribute to the Vietnam Airlift. Located next to the Welcome Center in Memorial Park. Dedicated in 1982.

Oceanport: Stone monument dedicated to area residents who served in Vietnam. Erected by V.F.W. Post 10129.

New Mexico

Angel Fire

Perched high on a hillside overlooking the magnificent Moreno Valley of Northern New Mexico is a sanctuary for quiet reflection. The Vietnam Veterans Peace and Brotherhood Chapel rests like a gull on the side of the mountains of the Sangre de Cristo range, surrounded by wildflowers of every hue. The chapel, near Angel Fire, was built in 1971 by Dr. Victor Westphall in memory of his son, David, who was killed by enemy ambush in Vietnam.

Dr. Westphall wanted us to remember his son and all the others who died in the war with pride and dignity and to pray that war would never have to take young lives again. He and his family built the simple chapel themselves. The triangular interior features a place for quiet meditation, with a single cross and a tall, narrow window at the apex. Opposite the apex is a wall of photos of Americans lost in the war.

After the chapel was dedicated, Dr. Westphall would close it each night, until one morning when he arrived to find a message from a young veteran scrawled across a board used to bar the door. It read, "I needed to come in and you locked me out." Since then the chapel has been open all hours, with special lighting added to illuminate the way.

By 1982 Dr. Westphall and his family could no longer manage the chapel alone, and the Disabled American Veterans formed an organization to assume the responsibility. They have since renamed the chapel the D.A.V. Vietnam Veterans National Memorial and have added a visitors center in order to display the memorabilia given to Dr. Westphall by grateful veterans and families.

Angel Fire, New Mexico: Three views of the D.A.V. Vietnam Veterans National Memorial, located near the town of Angel Fire in the Sangre de Cristo Mountains.

Cannon Air Force Base, New Mexico: Memorial to American P.O.W.s and M.I.A.s still in Southeast Asia.

Cannon Air Force Base

"God is Hope" reads the inscription on the memorial at Cannon Air Force Base in New Mexico, which is dedicated to American P.O.W.s and M.I.A.s still in Southeast Asia. The base of the monument is volcanic rock obtained from the Rio Grande Valley near Santa Fe. The inscription and large replica of a P.O.W./M.I.A. bracelet were designed by Chris Gikas. One of the earlier memorials, it was dedicated May 25, 1973, and stands as a reminder that hope is everything to those who wait.

Other New Mexico Memorials

Los Lunas: Park dedicated to Daniel Fernandez, Congressional Medal of Honor recipient.

New York

Glen Falls

Members of the Adirondack Chapter 70 of the Vietnam Veterans of America helped plan and raise funds for an impressive memorial, which was dedicated November 2, 1985. It is located at Adirondacks Community College in Glen Falls, New York. The engraved artwork on the jet-black granite is an outstanding tribute to the sacrifices made by Americans in Vietnam. It depicts a soldier praying over the vast field of headstones of his fallen friends.

New York City

From the battlefields of the war, without even knowing it, Vietnam veterans wrote their own memorial passages, to be etched years later into the glass block walls of the New York City Vietnam Veterans Memorial. Excerpts from eighty-three letters, mostly written by soldiers in combat, are engraved in the seventy-foot-long, sixteen-foot-high wall, which stands between South Street and Water Street in lower Manhattan.

During dedication ceremonies, May 6, 1985, Mayor Koch stirred the large crowd with these words: "We have heard the voices of a lost generation. We have opened the eyes of a new generation to the lessons of the past."

The "It's Time" parade held the following day through Broadway's "Route of Heroes" welcomed thousands of veterans home in a shower of tickertape.

Top: *New York, New York: The New York City Vietnam Veterans Memorial.* Bottom: *Plattsburgh, New York: Memorial at V.F.W. Post 125 commemorates every conflict in American history, including the American Revolution.*

Plattsburgh

American involvement in every conflict from the Revolutionary War to Beirut is remembered in the brick monument located at V.F.W. Post 125 in Plattsburgh, New York. It was designed by Ed Davis, a Navy veteran and recipient of the Navy Cross and the Purple Heart. He designed it to be symbolic of the Berlin Wall.

The two "graves" in front of the wall are in memory of the departed comrades. The two crosses are for the M.I.A.s and P.O.W.s. Names of those who served, including K.I.A., M.I.A., and living veterans, are on each of the 1,200 bricks that compose the wall. Eight flags fly behind the wall, one for each of the five branches of service, as well as the V.F.W., P.O.W./M.I.A., and American flags. This symbolic project was completed by Memorial Day, 1986.

Other New York Memorials

Albany: Memorial with names on a computer.

Buffalo: Memorial built in a semi-circular sloping wall.

Griffiss Air Force Base: Wooden bell tower dedicated to all Army Air Corps/Air Force Congressional Medal of Honor recipients. Also, a display board with pictures and information about the recipients. Located on Brooks Road. Dedicated Sept. 17, 1982.

New Rochelle: Monument dedicated to those who "sacrificed their lives for peace." Dedicated in 1969.

New York City: Flagpole on top of the World Trade Center. Dedicated to all Vietnam veterans.

Rosedale: Pedestal-type memorial with names listed.

West Point: Plaque installed on a boulder.

West Seneca: Block of granite etched with scenes of an American soldier and a map of Vietnam. Names of those lost are also listed.

North Carolina

Raleigh

North Carolina remembers its 206,000 Vietnam veterans, especially the 1,600 who died there and the sixty-one who are still missing. The North Carolina Vietnam Veterans Homecoming Salute was held May 22–24, 1987, to honor these veterans and to dedicate the state's new memorial located in Union Square, the State Capitol grounds in Raleigh. The memorial is an outstanding bronze sculpture by artist Abbe Godwin of Greensboro. The sculpture captures the likeness of two combat infantrymen carrying a wounded friend to a medivac. It realistically depicts the intensity of emotion in battle, as well as the compassion. The sculpture was cast at the Joel Meisner Foundry in Plainview, New York, the same foundry that cast Frederick Hart's statue "The Three Fighting Men" located across from "The Wall" in Washington, D.C.

Near the sculpture are five nine-inch bronze plaques with the emblems of the five branches of the armed services, along with a gray granite dedication plaque. The plaque reads, "Dedicated to the men and women of North Carolina who served with dignity and honor in the Vietnam War. May 23, 1987."

At this time the memorial committee hopes to build a moving wall with the names of all those who died or are still missing, which will travel around the state, then become a permanent part of the memorial. They also would like to add lighting and granite benches to the site. A documentary on the making of this memorial may be yet produced.

On the first Saturday of each month, at noon, the names of the dead and missing are read by volunteer groups from across the state at the memorial site. In this way, North Carolina continues to remember its heroes.

Raleigh, North Carolina: Bronze sculpture on State Capitol grounds commemorates North Carolinians who served in Vietnam.

Also in Raleigh are a living memorial for P.O.W./M.I.A.s at the Boy Scout Headquarters; a living memorial at the Bicentennial Plaza; a memorial on the lawn of the Museum of History; and a bronze plaque at Oakwood Cemetery in the House of Memory.

Seymour Johnson Air Force Base

A lone magnolia tree stands as a reminder of a friend who has not yet returned home. The plaque in front of the tree tells of the reason the tree was planted. It reads:

Seymour Johnson Air Force Base, North Carolina: The Freedom Tree.

The Freedom Tree
With the vision of universal freedom
for all mankind
this tree is dedicated to
Capt. Samuel Cornelius
and all
Prisoners of War
and
Missing in Action
1974

This Freedom Tree stands in front of the Officers Open Mess at Seymour Johnson Air Force Base in Goldsboro, North Carolina. Captain Cornelius was a pilot with the 336th Tactical Fighter Squadron there. He was downed on June 16, 1973, in Southeast Asia. His friends everywhere still pray for his return.

Also on Seymour Johnson Air Force Base, in the shadow of an F-105 Thunderchief, stands another P.O.W./M.I.A. memorial. This monument was donated by chief master sergeants at the base. Aircrews of the Fourth Tactical Fighter Wing at Seymour Johnson flew the F-105 and F-4 aircrafts

Seymour Johnson Air Force Base, N.C.: P.O.W./M.I.A. memorial stands beneath a mounted F-105 Thunderchief.

on missions during the war. The memorial on the base was dedicated May 27, 1983.

Other North Carolina Memorials

Asheville: Plaque.

Bolivia: Honor Roll of Valor.

Brevard: Marble monument.

Charlotte: Proposed memorial site.

Durham: Proposed memorial site.

Ft. Bragg: (1) Granite monument for P.O.W./M.I.A.s. Located on the main parade grounds. (2) Bronze sculpture, Special Forces memorial.

Goldsboro: Marker honoring those men and women who served and those who died. Located in Herman Park.

Greensboro: Plaque on the Courthouse.

Greenville: Granite memorial with names of those killed in action.

Halifax: Plaque in the Courthouse with names of those killed in action.

Havelock: Flagpole at a high school.

Jefferson: Plaque inside the Courthouse.

Lillington: Plaque installed at the Courthouse honoring Vietnam veterans.

Lincolnton: Monument to those lost in the war.

Littleton: Plaque and flagpole.

Morganton: Monument with names of those killed or missing in the war; also plaque.

Murphy: Three granite stones listing names of those killed or missing.

Newton: Bronze plaque on Courthouse for county residents lost in the war.

Oxford: (1) Plaque on the Federal Building dedicated to Vietnam veterans killed in action. (2) Memorial plaque in J.F. Webb High School for graduates killed in action in Vietnam. (3) Plaque and flagpole at Mens' Garden Club Park.

Robbinsville: Monument in a marble plaza.

Rocky Mount: Marble monument with an eagle.

Roxboro: Memorial plaque at the Courthouse.

Smithfield: Memorial located on the Courthouse grounds honoring Vietnam veterans.

Statesville: Monument in front of the Courthouse listing all those lost in the war.

Taylorsville: Monument to those lost in the war.

Transylvania County: Marble monument dedicated to those killed or missing in the war.

Waynesville: Monument in front of Courthouse.

Wilson: Plaque on the Courthouse.

Winston-Salem: Memorial of over 58,000 bricks, one for each of the people who died or are missing from the war.

North Dakota

Bismarck: Proposed statewide memorial on the Capitol grounds.

Fargo: Memorial of individual bricks engraved with the names of all those killed, missing, or disabled because of the war.

New Town, Fort Berthold Reservation: Memorial to all veterans of Vietnam.

Other memorials are located in Rugby and Mandan.

Ohio

Circleville

Time and time again, Vietnam veterans of Circleville, Ohio, were turned down by local officials in their quest to erect a memorial to their fallen comrades. Because there were no memorials to veterans of earlier wars, they were told to honor them first or incorporate them into their memorial.

A privately owned piece of land adjoining Ted Lewis Park was finally located and donated to the veterans by Mr. Ed Bermile. The circular memorial, which displays photos as well as names of twenty-five Americans lost in Vietnam, was dedicated November 12, 1983.

Circleville, Ohio: Circleville Vietnam Veterans Memorial.

158

Other Ohio Memorials

Bay Village: Plaque in Veterans Memorial Rose Garden with photos and a biography of a local high school graduate who served in Vietnam.

Bellefontaine: Monument of granite, listing names of those killed and missing.

Canton: Statue with inscribed plaque.

Dayton: Vietnam Veterans Memorial Park, a living memorial with walkways, flowers and trees. A large granite monument is engraved with names of those killed or missing. Located on the east bank of the Miami River, south of Stewart Street Bridge. Dedicated May 26, 1986.

Glouster: Monument or marble and granite.

Harding County: Thirteen marble disks laid in granite paving. Each disk represents a local casualty of the war.

Mansillon: Marble monument with inscription.

Marion: Map of Vietnam and an inscription on a granite monument.

Utica: Flagpole dedicated to Vietnam veterans.

Other memorials are located in the following cities:

Cambridge
Cincinnati
Newton Falls
Sylvania
Toledo
Warren

Oklahoma

Oklahoma City

Mike Mullings returned home from the 1982 dedication of the National Vietnam Veterans Memorial in Washington, D.C., with a fierce determination to help build a memorial to his fellow Vietnam veterans in his own home state of Oklahoma. He thought a statue on the State Capitol grounds in Oklahoma City would be just what was needed. So he worked for almost two years lobbying the State Legislature for support of his idea. Finally, in May of 1983, legislation was passed that far exceeded Mike's hopes.

The state agreed to help develop and set aside land for the Oklahoma Veterans Memorial Garden, which will honor not only the Vietnam veterans, but also veterans of both the World Wars and Korea. Each of the four time periods will include its own statue in a landscaped setting. It has been agreed that $150,000 will be paid for each statue placed in the park. The first statue to be erected will be that of a soldier for the Vietnam period. The eight-foot-high statue will sit atop a base that lists the names of the deceased and missing Oklahomans. The other statues will follow, each one with its own dedication date and ceremony. The garden, when finished, will take up the entire north lawn of the Capitol grounds and will be an excellent tribute to all veterans of the state of Oklahoma. With a strong belief in what he was doing, and with the help of his fellow Oklahomans, Mike Mullings succeeded in seeing his dream come true.

Oregon

Beaverton

One of the earliest memorials was actually started in the early sixties by Buck Janigan, a member of Beaverton, Oregon, Elks Lodge 1989. Mr. Janigan had lost a son, Cpl. Richard A. Janigan, in the war in Vietnam. It was completed and dedicated by Governor Tom L. McCall on June 9, 1968. For many years it was the only Vietnam memorial in the state of Oregon.

In 1983, separate black marble slabs were added to record the names of all Oregon residents who died in the war. The back side of the memorial includes a large mosaic mural of an elk designed by Newman Myrah, a fellow Elks Lodge member. The memorial is located on the grounds of the Elks Lodge in Beaverton.

Portland

The "Living Memorial" in Portland remembers the sacrifices made by more than 57,000 men and women of Oregon who served, died, or remain captive in Vietnam. The moving, many-faceted tribute is part of the Hoyt Arboretum. It consists of a winding walkway which begins under a 160-foot-long, vine-covered pergola, leads into a central meadow with a reflecting pool and water stairs, then proceeds to a widening circular path with glass walls engraved with the names of the 659 killed in Vietnam, and ends finally with the "Missing in Action" memorial and a full view of Mt. Hood.

Beaverton, Oregon: Top: *The Richard A. Janigan Vietnam Veterans Memorial.*
Bottom: *Mosaic on the back of the Richard A. Janigan Memorial.*

Other Oregon Memorials

Albany: Plaques on rock wall listing names of those killed in action. Located in Timber Linn Memorial Park.

The Dalles: Flagpole and base. Base is inscribed with names of men killed in Vietnam from the mid–Columbia region. Located at Kelly Viewpoint near Sconnis Park, overlooking the Dalles and the Columbia Gorge.

Hermiston: Stone monument with bronze plaque and flagpole.

Hood River: Bronze plaque located on Courthouse.

Independence: Flagpole and monument.

Klamath Falls: Brass plaque listing names of those killed in action. Located in Courthouse square.

Newport: Marble slab with eternal flame. Located on Courthouse lawn.

Rogue River: Wood and brass monument with inscription. Located on Highway 99 beside the Rogue River.

Pennsylvania

Beaver County

For over seven months the *Beaver County Times*, obviously a small town paper with a big heart, kept their readers updated on the fundraising drive they were sponsoring for the Beaver County Vietnam Veterans Memorial. The paper continuously ran large ads asking, "They cared – do you?" Touching stories from families who'd lost members in Southeast Asia were also featured, often accompanied by pictures of smiling young faces which never grew old.

Meeting their goal in just months, Carl Fleeson, chairman of the memorial committee and promotion manager of the paper, and others were proud to attend the dedication ceremonies on November 11, 1983.

Berwick

In the spring of 1983 a unique tribute was dedicated in Briar Creek Lake Park, Columbia County, near Berwick, Pennsylvania. Eleven small bronze plaques, each with the name of an area veteran who died in Vietnam, were placed near the bases of eleven hemlock trees, arranged in a semicircle in the park. Hemlock trees were chosen as they are the state tree of Pennsylvania. A larger bronze plaque with an inscription reading, "Columbia County Heroes of Vietnam," rests in front of a very tall flagstaff in the semicircle.

V.F.W. and American Legion members took part and provided a firing

Opposite: *Beaver County, Pennsylvania: The Beaver County Vietnam Veterans Memorial.*

Top: *Beaver County, Pennsylvania: Fundraising ad appearing in the Beaver County Times shows sketch of Beaver County Vietnam Veterans Memorial. The words "And those who remain missing in action" were added to the center column of the actual monument.* Bottom: *Berwick, Pennsylvania: Site in Briar Creek Lake Park where eleven hemlock trees, planted in a semicircle, are dedicated to Columbia County area veterans who died in Vietnam.*

Berwick, Pennsylvania: Top: *Hemlock tree and dedicatory plaque are part of Columbia County's tribute to Vietnam veterans. Each of eleven trees is dedicated to a local resident killed in Southeast Asia.* Bottom: *Close-up of one of the dedicatory plaques.*

squad and buglers for the dedication ceremony. Representatives of the county soil conservation service and the Veterans Administration helped plan the event, along with David Champ, the park director.

Doylestown, Pennsylvania: Two views of the Bucks County Vietnam Veterans Memorial.

Doylestown

The courtyard of the Courthouse in Doylestown, Pennsylvania, is the location of a large, impressive memorial to Vietnam veterans. A curved wall bearing more than 130 names of Bucks County residents who served in the war is the focal point of the circular plaza. The memorial was dedicated on June 16, 1984, with a parade and ceremony. The inscription on the curved wall reads, "To remember and honor those Americans who gave of themselves in the Vietnam War."

Private funding for the tribute was obtained by the Bucks County Vietnam War Memorial Fund, Inc., led by Dan Fraley. The winning design for the memorial was submitted by Diseroad & Wolff architectural firm.

Indiana

Considering that many college campuses were the sites for student demonstrations against the war, the idea of a Vietnam veterans memorial on a college campus may be unusual, but certainly not impossible. One such idea originated with Marine veteran Robert Gault, who had served as the president of the Veterans Club of Indiana University of Pennsylvania, and wished to see such a memorial on that campus.

He enlisted the help of the Veterans Club, the administration of the university, the military science and Army R.O.T.C. departments, Bill Kegel of the R & P Coal Company, and others to design and build a fitting tribute. The memorial, which was dedicated on November 11, 1982, is located between Keith Hall and Leonard Hall. It is surrounded by oak and cherry trees, shrubbery, and benches. It was designed to be a quiet place of meditation. The bronze plaque reads:

> In honor of the patriotic men and women who served their country in the Vietnam War and in memory of those who made the supreme sacrifice.

Johnstown

They asked the sculptor to carve a child in the soldier's arms, rather than a gun, to remind us of the kindness shown by so many American soldiers to the children of war. And so he stands today in Johnstown, Pennsylvania, a "typical" soldier, rescuing a small child. Two Gold Star Mothers, Margaret Seigrist and Louise Gaven, conceived the idea for a veteran's park and recruited family, friends, and their community to help. They ordered the statue to made in this manner, and in accordance with the authentic uniform and equipment details they had carefully researched.

Vincent Illuzzi of Barre, Vermont, spent two years creating the statue, which recognizes all veterans and was dedicated Memorial Day, 1974.

Top: *Indiana, Pennsylvania: Vietnam Veterans Memorial on the campus of Indiana University of Pennsylvania.* Bottom: *Johnstown, Pennsylvania: Statue honoring all American veterans stands in a veterans park in Johnstown.*

Mercer County, Pennsylvania: The Mercer County Vietnam Veterans Memorial (front view, left; rear view, right).

Mercer County

Members of the Mercer County, Pennsylvania, Vietnam Era Veterans Association, with the help of such celebrities as Gen. William C. Westmoreland and former Pittsburgh Steeler and Vietnam veteran Rocky Bleier, raised over $6,000 for their monument. The Pennsylvania black granite column bears the names of thirty-nine area residents lost in combat. The monument is located on the Courthouse lawn in Mercer. It was dedicated in ceremonies on December 11, 1983, with Gen. Westmoreland as featured speaker.

Sheffield

In October of 1975, the small town of Sheffield, Pennsylvania, honored one of its finest sons, Army Staff Sgt. John G. Gertsch, by dedicating a new sports complex at the county high school to his name. Col. Harold A. Polson, his battalion commander in Vietnam, was the guest of honor at the dedication ceremony. Col. Polson describes his friend, Sgt. Gertsch, as one of the 101st Airborne Division's bravest troopers, with a legendary reputation throughout the division as a man who knew no fear.

During his second tour of duty in Northern I Corps, Vietnam, in July of 1969, Sgt. Gertsch unselfishly gave his life to protect an aidman who was treating a wounded officer by rushing forward and positioning himself between them and the enemy. For this last gallant act, and for the way that Sgt. Gertsch had led his troops, while wounded and under heavy enemy attack, in the preceding days, he was awarded the Congressional Medal of Honor (posthumously).

Col. Polson said of Sgt. Gertsch:

> No one person that I have known in three wars deserved the Medal of Honor more than John, for it was not just the exploits depicted during the period 15–19 July 1969, there were numerous other episodes where he had demonstrated previously the courage and devotion to his men that made him an inspirational leader and a man I shall be eternally proud to have known.

The dedication of the sports complex was just part of a memorable weekend for the town of Sheffield. It included half-time ceremonies at the football game and a parade through town, proudly led by the 101st Airborne Division Band and Color Guard from Ft. Campbell, Kentucky. A large banquet was also held that evening. Sheffield proudly remembers a young boy who grew up in an orphans' home and went on to receive our nation's highest honor by giving his life to help others.

Other Pennsylvania Memorials

Butler: Six-foot black granite monument listing names of county residents killed in the Vietnam War. Located in Diamond Park. Dedicated November 11, 1983.

Carlisle: Veterans Memorial Courtyard. Located at High and Hanover streets. Dedicated May 1983.

Coudersport: Podium-type monument constructed on granite. Located behind the Courthouse.

Harrisburg: Granite monument dedicated to all Vietnam veterans. Erected by the V.N.V.M.C.

Kittanning: Granite monument dedicated to Vietnam veterans of Armstrong County. Located in River Front Park. Dedicated November 7, 1981.

Pittsburgh: Proposed memorial will be built on the north shore of the Allegheny River beside Three Rivers Stadium. Designed to be an open-air dome.

Scranton: Granite monument dedicated to those who served in Vietnam. Located at the Courthouse Square. Dedicated in 1977.

Wilkinsburg: Six-foot-high concrete tablets with black marble center. Located in front of Wilkinsburg Borough Building. Dedicated 1983.

Wormleysburg: American Legion State Headquarters had a statue dedicated to Vietnam veterans.

Rhode Island

Exeter: "V"-shaped monument made from eleven slabs of granite. Names of those killed and missing in action are engraved.

Providence: Proposed honor roll of all veterans to be located in the State House Rotunda.

South Carolina

Columbia

The fight for freedom is a South Carolina tradition. Citizens there have participated in all nine major wars. To honor the veterans of our nation's longest war, South Carolina has dedicated a beautiful native granite memorial in the capital city of Columbia.

The focal point of the South Carolina Vietnam Veterans Monument is the towering, pylon carved with frieze designs depicting each branch of the armed services in Vietnam. It is topped with a powerful light which acts as a beacon, honoring all those who served. The pylon is flanked by two large granite walls on which are listed the names of 885 South Carolinians who never came home from the war. The names are arranged in order by counties, so that this is also a community memorial.

The Vietnam Veterans of South Carolina, Inc., was formed in 1983, in part to help build a state memorial. They had been inspired by the dedication in 1982 of the National Vietnam Veterans Memorial in Washington, D.C. A monument committee was also formed later, in 1985. The design for the monument was submitted by Allen Marshall of the Columbia Architectural Group, Inc. The theme he chose reflects on the great sacrifices that the war demanded of its participants. Patrick Killey, a graphics designer with South Carolina Educational Television, was chosen to create the frieze designs. A site was chosen in downtown Congaree Vista Park. The monument is surrounded by landscaping and benches.

An entire "Veterans Weekend" of events and ceremonies was held to dedicate the monument November 7–11, 1986. The weekend included an interfaith memorial service, a sunrise service, and an all-night prayer vigil with a reading of the names on the monument. The dedication ceremony on November 8 was followed by an Army National Guard Band concert

175

Greenville, South Carolina: The Greenville County Vietnam Veterans Monument, shown as model (top) and actual monument (bottom).

Opposite: *Columbia, South Carolina: The South Carolina Vietnam Veterans Monument.*

in the afternoon and an evening retreat and lighting ceremony. A reception by the Vietnam Veterans of South Carolina, Inc., was held that night. A musical tribute at the memorial was performed November 9, by the South Carolina Philharmonic Orchestra. The long weekend was finally concluded on November 11 with the annual Veterans Day Parade, which was led by Gen. William C. Westmoreland.

Greenville

The Greenville County Vietnam Veterans Monument was dedicated on November 7, 1987. The citizens who worked on the fundraising drive hope to raise awareness of the contributions that veterans have made to this nation. The monument is located in Cleveland Park, adjacent to the Anderson Memorial. More than 100 names of war casualties are listed on the black granite panels of the "V"-shaped memorial.

Other South Carolina Memorials

Charleston Air Force Base: Six-foot-high monument of granite. Located near the Wing Headquarters. Dedicated November 3, 1983.

South Dakota

Springfield

The Veterans Memorial Plaza, located in Springfield, South Dakota, was finished in October of 1972. The memorial consists of several large concrete forms, with water flowing out over the top form and then collecting

Springfield, South Dakota: Veterans Memorial Plaza, dedicated to all United States veterans.

Springfield, South Dakota: Dedicatory plaque at Veterans Memorial Plaza.

at the base in a small pool. Members of the Veterans Club of the University of South Dakota helped plan and raise money for the plaza, which honors veterans of all wars. Funding came from several raffles held by the Veterans Club along with donations from various veterans organizations and private citizens.

Watertown

The Codington County Vietnam Veterans Memorial was dedicated Veterans Day, 1985, with well over 1,000 people present, despite the first storm of winter. It was the first such memorial in South Dakota, and is located in front of the Courthouse in Watertown.

Watertown, South Dakota: The Codington County Vietnam Veterans Memorial.

All of the money to pay for the project was raised locally. Most of the work, including the shaping and engraving of the stone, was done by veterans. They also did the site work, including the foundation and concrete, and installed the granite slabs themselves.

The poem "Soldier" by George Skypeck, as well as some of Mr. Skypeck's excellent artwork, appear on the black granite markers. This granite was the same used in the National Vietnam Veterans Memorial in Washington, D.C. The gray granite of the benches came from quarries in South Dakota.

Other South Dakota Memorials

Pierre: (1) Plaque listing all those missing in action from South Dakota. Located in the State Capitol. (2) Proposed state monument consisting of granite slabs, with all names engraved, and a flame.

Pine Ridge: Monument of marble with names of Vietnam veterans.

Sioux Falls: Proposed monument to veterans of Minnehaha County.

Tennessee

Athens

The Honorable Marvin S. Bolinger, mayor of the city of Athens, Tennessee, and a company commander of Company C, 1/502 Infantry, 101st Airborne Division, from October 1970 to September 1971, is very proud of the fine Vietnam memorial in his city. The white granite monolith, presented to the city by the local unit of the Woodmen of the World, is located on a plaza in front of the Athens Municipal Building on North Jackson Street. It stands adjacent to a similar monument dedicated to Korea veterans. The tribute is engraved with the names of eighteen McMinn county residents who died in Vietnam.

Knoxville

One of the earliest and most striking memorials stands on the front lawn of the City and County Building in Knoxville, Tennessee. It was originally designed and built in only two weeks in 1973. The proud white eagle was later destroyed in a nearby construction accident. It then took three years to restore and rededicate the memorial, with new plaques bearing the names of 205 war dead from surrounding counties.

Milan

"A lasting tribute to our fallen heroes" is how Mayor Herb Davis described the gleaming new Veterans War Memorial in Milan, Tennessee. During the dedication ceremonies on November 10, 1985, the mayor

Top: *Athens, Tennessee: Athens Vietnam Veterans Memorial.* Bottom: *Knoxville, Tennessee: Knoxville Vietnam Veterans Memorial.*

Milan, Tennessee: Milan Veterans War Memorial, dedicated to those who died in World War I, World War II, Korea, and Vietnam.

thanked the many citizens and organizations that helped raise the needed $12,000 in just six months. Danny Hopper, who proudly served with the United States Marine Corps in Vietnam in 1968 and 1969, conceived the idea for the monument. Rankin Mathis, Jr., was the general chairperson for the fundraising group.

The massive granite monument was built by the Greenfield Monument Works. It is over seven feet high and eight feet wide, weighing 22,000 pounds. It bears the names of thirty-six area persons who died in our nation's wars.

Nashville

The Tennessee Vietnam Veterans Leadership Program, calling for a time to remember the great personal sacrifices made by Americans in

Nashville, Tennessee: Statue to be included in Tennessee's State Vietnam Veterans Memorial.

Vietnam, is sponsoring a memorial fund to erect a monument on the State Capitol grounds in Nashville, Tennessee. It will include a statue of three infantrymen on patrol and the names of the 1,287 Tennesseeans who died in the war. Plans are also to preserve a scroll of the names of all donors, to be locked into the base of the monument and opened in the year 2085.

Somerville

Representatives of the Fayette County Historical Society, the local V.F.W., the American Legion, the city of Somerville, and the Tennessee

Somerville, Tennessee: Fayette County Veterans Memorial honors all American veterans.

National Guard all worked together to fund and erect an impressive veterans memorial. It is located on the Courthouse grounds in Somerville, Tennessee.

The dedication of the monument was held November 11, 1984, and included a public ceremony and display of military service memorabilia. The twelve-foot, Georgia granite pillar is a tribute to sacrifices made by Americans who served in all wars from the Revolution through Vietnam.

Other Tennessee Memorials

Chattanooga: Veterans Bridge, crossing the Tennessee River, from Barton Avenue to Georgia Avenue.

Madisonville: Vietnam veterans monument.

Texas

Austin

Members of the Austin Chapter of the Military Order of the World Wars helped plan and raise funding for the Vietnam War Memorial, which was dedicated May 26, 1980. It is located in Waterloo Park in Austin, Texas, a few blocks east of the State Capitol.

The monument is constructed of stainless steel and has a five-point star on top. It is surrounded by stone walkways and red roses. More than 100 names of those killed are on metal plaques set flat on the concrete base of the memorial. It is a bold and fitting tribute to the sacrifices made by Austin and Travis County citizens who served and died in Southeast Asia.

Carswell Air Force Base

The officers and airmen who flew and supported B-52 and KC-135 operations during the war in Southeast Asia are honored with a brick and granite monument at Carswell Air Force Base in Texas. The monument was dedicated May 9, 1975. It is located outside of Base Operations and faces the flight line. It was presented by the V.F.W. Post 8235 and Auxiliary.

El Paso

Bright gold mums filled in the large concrete outline of a star at the site of the El Paso, Texas, Veterans Memorial. It was the Bicentennial project of the local Gold Star Mothers chapter.

President Gerald Ford dedicated the monument before a crowd of

Top: *Carswell Air Force Base, Texas: Monument to officers and airmen of B-52 and KC-135 operations in Southeast Asia.* Bottom: *El Paso, Texas: Dedication ceremonies for the El Paso County Veterans Memorial. President Gerald Ford stands at left.*

El Paso, Texas: Top: *Dedicatory plaque at the El Paso County Veterans Memorial.* Bottom: *Granite marker at the El Paso County Veterans Memorial bears the names of local residents who died in Vietnam.*

Gold Star Mothers, local dignitaries, and citizens in the spring of 1976. The granite stone in front of the star bears the names of those from El Paso

Longview, Texas: Memorial to all Gregg County veterans is topped by a statue of a soldier in Vietnam-era uniform.

County who died or are still missing in Southeast Asia. A bronze plaque reads, "In memory of our sons who gave their lives in defense of our country."

Randolph Air Force Base, Texas: "Missing Man Monument," dedicated to all Americans lost in Southeast Asia.

Longview

"Served With Honor" is the title of a six-foot-tall bronze statue in Longview, Texas. The striking likeness of a soldier dressed in Vietnam-era uniform was sculpted by Neil Logan. The memorial to all area veterans stands on the grounds of the new Gregg County Courthouse addition.

One bronze plaque attached to the base of the statue reads: "In honored memory of all Gregg County veterans of all wars, living and dead." The plaque is also engraved with the symbols of all five branches of service. Another plaque contains the "Veterans Communion."

Randolph Air Force Base

For many years airmen have flown the "Missing Man Formation" as a tribute to those lost in battle. On March 4, 1977, the San Antonio Chapter of the Red River Valley Fighter Pilots Association dedicated their own Missing Man Monument, a 25-foot aluminum and steel version of the famous formation, to all Americans lost in Southeast Asia during the war.

San Antonio, Texas: "Hill 881," the Vietnam veterans memorial in San Antonio.

The members of the association and wives of the P.O.W.s and M.I.A.s raised the money for this magnificent memorial by selling thousands of P.O.W./M.I.A. bracelets. The sculpture stands beside Building 100 (known as the Taj Mahal) on Randolph Air Force Base in Texas. It was created by Mark Pritchett of Helotes, Texas.

Across the base is written:

We who came home must never forget those who could not.

San Antonio

"Hill 881" is the title of the Vietnam veterans memorial in San Antonio, Texas. It depicts a soldier leaning over to give aid to a wounded buddy. The

San Marcos, Texas: Marker at Veterans Memorial Park, dedicating the park to those who died in Vietnam.

battle on Hill 881 was one of the fiercest in Vietnam. Many American lives were lost on that hill. The statue was dedicated in November of 1986, with a huge crowd in attendance. It is located in front of the Municipal Auditorium.

San Marcos

The city of San Marcos, Texas, in 1976, dedicated Rincon Park to those residents who lost their lives in Vietnam. The park was at that time renamed Veterans Memorial Park. At the entrance to the park, which is located on Rincon Street, is a permanent monument and plaque placed there by the Urban Renewal Board of Commissioners. The plaque bears the names of twelve area residents who died in the war. The park contains much unique playground equipment for local youngsters to enjoy.

Other Texas Memorials

Dallas: Granite monument located in a park. Dedicated to all those killed or missing in the war.

Laughlin Air Force Base: Granite monument with inscription. Dedicated to all P.O.W./M.I.A.s on July 19, 1985.

Reese Air Force Base: Monument dedicated to all those missing in action. Dedicated April 4, 1976.

Sheppard Air Force Base: Monument dedicated to all those missing in action.

Utah

Salt Lake City: Proposed eight-foot statue to be located on the Capitol grounds. Planned dedication to be July 4, 1988.

Vermont

Sharon

The state of Vermont dedicated Interstate 89 as Veterans Memorial Highway on October 30, 1982. A twelve-foot-high granite monument, listing the names of 138 citizens of Vermont who lost their lives in Vietnam, is located in a rest area along the highway in the town of Sharon.

The dedication was attended by several hundred veterans and their families as well as dignitaries, including Governor Richard Snelling and Lieutenant Governor Madeleine Kunin.

Virginia

Alleghany County

Twenty-seven citizens of Alleghany County, Virginia, lost their lives in the Vietnam and Korean wars combined. Their heroic sacrifices are jointly remembered in a striking monument in Covington, Virginia. Special permission had to be obtained to reproduce the Congressional Medal of Honor on the bronze plaque. The medal was bestowed upon two area residents, Michael Fleming Folland and Gary Lee Miller, who both served in Vietnam. The inscription below the names reads simply, "From Those Who Care... Nov. 11, 1982."

Little Creek

There were 252 men killed while serving in the Navy's River Patrol Force in Vietnam. These brave Americans were honored with an imposing obelisk dedicated in July of 1980. The Gamewardens of Vietnam, a national organization of veterans who served on the river boats in Vietnam, established this memorial on the Naval Amphibious Base in Little Creek, Virginia. The names of the dead are engraved on the sides of the monument along with the division or teams they worked with. Around the base are engraved the names of their areas of operations in Vietnam.

Richmond

On November 20, 1981, an addition to the impressive Virginia War Memorial in Richmond was dedicated to recognize those lost in the

Alleghany County, Virginia: Monument to those who died in Korea and Vietnam.

Little Creek, Virginia: Memorial on the Naval Amphibious Base in Little Creek honors men killed while serving on the Navy's River Patrol Force in Vietnam.

Richmond, Virginia: The Virginia War Memorial includes a special tribute to Vietnam veterans.

Vietnam War. This memorial was originally dedicated in 1956 to commemorate the service and sacrifices of Virginians in World War II and Korea. The addition included glass panels engraved with the names of the deceased. These panels are located in the center of the building itself, between what is called the "Shrine of Memory" and the adjacent 200-seat memorial auditorium.

The focal point of the large "Shrine of Memory" is a majestic white marble statue entitled "Memory," which symbolizes Virginia womanhood gazing with pride and sorrow on the names of the fallen warriors. The "Torch of Liberty," an eternal flame, burns near the base of the statue.

A very unique part of this tribute is the "Memorial Coffers," which are embedded in the floor of the shrine. These coffers contain authentic war relics and mementoes from throughout the world. The Vietnam section contains such things as a cartridge belt, a Purple Heart, grenade fragments, a North Vietnamese belt and buckle, a canteen cover, a M-16 clip magazine, pungee sticks, camouflage face paint, a beret with insignia, and the identification plate from a Huey helicopter.

A special invitation to visit Virginia's memorials is extended to all veterans by Governor Charles S. Robb, who proudly served as a Marine officer in Vietnam, under the leadership of his father-in-law, the late President Lyndon B. Johnson.

Virginia Beach

The bronze plaque on the "Flame of Hope" memorial at Naval Air Station Oceana, Virginia Beach, Virginia, is inscribed with these words:

> This flame will burn continuously to light the way for the return of our prisoners of war held in Southeast Asia.

And so it has since its dedication in 1972, despite public apathy and the energy crisis of the 1970s. In 1973, because of financial problems, the flame itself was transferred by candle to Oceana's Chapel of the Good Shepherd. The memorial itself was then topped with a bronze replica of the flame.

Virginia Beach, Virginia: Relighting ceremony for the "Flame of Hope" Memorial at Naval Air Station Oceana at Virginia Beach.

Virginia Beach, Virginia: The "Flame of Hope" Memorial symbolizes hope for the return of all P.O.W.s in Southeast Asia.

The flame remained in the chapel for eleven years, until March of 1984, when a fundraising drive led by Mrs. Jill Seay and the Virginia Beach Jaycees brought the flame back to its place of honor atop the memorial. There it waits for all the Americans to come home.

Other Virginia Memorials

Colonial Heights: Addition to a granite wing to an existing veterans monument.

Danville: Monument to Vietnam and Korea veterans.

Fork Union: Bronze marker to those killed in action in the war. Located at the Fork Union Military Academy, in the academy chapel.

Radford: Granite marker and flagpole.

Washington

McChord Air Force Base

McChord Air Force Base in the state of Washington has a monument dedicated to all airmen and to all those listed as Missing in Action or Prisoners of War. Dedicated March 28, 1972, it is located at the entrance to the Fourth MAS Building.

Seattle

The Washington Memorial Plaza was established in 1951. It is located along the outside of the Public Safety Building in downtown Seattle. The names of the Vietnam and Korean War dead were placed on the memorial in 1975. A campaign to raise the funds to add these names was led by Joseph Feldman, adjutant of the American Legion Post 1 in Seattle. This memorial wall lists 1,001 names of Washingtonians who gave their lives in Vietnam.

Spokane

The Inland Empire Vietnam Veterans Memorial Fund raised $80,000 to pay for its memorial in Riverfront Park, in downtown Spokane, Washington. The bronze statue of an American fighting man was dedicated on November 10, 1985. On the base of the statue are those names of soldiers from Spokane County killed in Vietnam. Part of the dedication reads, ". . . to those who served and to those who gave their lives and are now in the hands of God."

McChord Air Force Base, Washington: Monument dedicated to all airmen, M.I.A.s, and P.O.W.s.

Other Washington Memorials

Everson: Proposed memorial building.

Olympia: Addition to existing monument that will be dedicated to Vietnam veterans, with a list of those killed or missing in action.

West Virginia

Charleston

West Virginia has sent a higher percentage of her young people to serve in the defense of our nation than any other state. As a result, she has suffered more casualties and received more medals for valor than any other state, on a per capita basis. To honor those veterans and their service to their country, the people of the state have dedicated themselves to building an outstanding Veterans Memorial Plaza on the Capitol grounds in Charleston. A Vietnam Veterans Memorial Commission was established by the state legislature in 1985 to assist in this effort.

The memorial itself will be composed of four separate monoliths, forming an oval, with an interior sanctuary. Each monolith will represent one of the four major wars of this century: World War I, World War II, Korea, and Vietnam. On the exterior wall of each monolith will be an alcove, which will house a bronze sculpture of a member of the armed services representative of that conflict. Surrounding the entire memorial will be an oval reflecting pool. Four ramped bridges will extend over the water into the interior of the memorial. Each bridge will lead from the memorial out to four separate memorial parks, which will include educational and historical material about that particular period in history.

Although the memorial will be completed at one point in time, each monument will be separately dedicated in order to pay tribute to those veterans with the placement of each bronze sculpture. The first monolith to be dedicated is scheduled to be the Vietnam Veterans Memorial on November 11, 1988. This memorial will be the only one to have a listing of the names of the deceased and missing inscribed.

It has been over fifty years since there has been a statewide veterans monument built in West Virginia, the last one being built to honor Civil

Charleston, West Virginia: Model of proposed state memorial to veterans of World War I, World War II, Korea, and Vietnam.

War veterans. The state has now decided to make up for that long period by building a truly magnificent tribute to its many heroes.

Other West Virginia Monuments

Middlebourne: Stone monument at the Courthouse.
New Martinsville: Stone monument at the War Memorial Building.
St. Marys: Stone monument at the Courthouse.

Wisconsin

Algoma

Another early Vietnam memorial is located at the intersection of State Highways 42 and 54, near Algoma, Wisconsin. The Algoma Optimist Club erected the brick monument and tall flagstaff in 1969. It was dedicated to Algoma area residents who served and died in Vietnam. The war itself was to last another six long years.

Hudson

Eighty percent of the donations given to fund the Veterans Memorial on the Courthouse lawn in Hudson, Wisconsin, were for five dollars or less, according to Lee Kellaher, the vice chairman of the fundraising committee. And yet the total of $10,000 was raised in a little over six months, with the combined help of the V.F.W., American Legion, Amvets, Disabled Veterans, the St. Croix County Board, and other organizations and individuals. In fact, the committee raised an additional $4,000 beyond the cost of the monument. The money will all be used for county projects honoring veterans.

Nearly 200 people attended the dedication of the black granite memorial to all St. Croix County veterans on May 19, 1984. All branches of the armed forces were represented in the combined services color guard at the dedication. The flags of each of the five branches are flown behind the monument, with the American flag flown above and to the left.

Top: *Algoma, Wisconsin: Memorial to Algoma area Vietnam veterans. This monument is topped by a flagpole.* Bottom: *Hudson, Wisconsin: Dedication ceremonies for the St. Croix County memorial, dedicated to all area veterans.*

Oconomowoc, Wisconsin: Memorial to all who served in Korea and Vietnam.

Milwaukee

The Milwaukee County War Memorial Center houses a Vietnam Honor Roll reflecting pool on its first level. The reflecting pool is surrounded by flat granite squares engraved with the names of area residents who died in the war. The symbols of the four branches of service are depicted in mosaic tile above the pool itself.

Oconomowoc

In a park overlooking LacLaBelle in downtown Oconomowoc, Wisconsin, is a solemn monument to all who served in both Korea and Vietnam. It was dedicated in 1983 and built by local veterans and concerned citizens.

Other Wisconsin Memorials

Fort Atkinson: Monument located at a high school.
Janesville: Stone marker located downtown. Dedicated to Korean and Vietnam veterans.

Wyoming

Cheyenne

The Veterans Administration Medical and Regional Office Center in Cheyenne, Wyoming, is the site of the Wyoming Vietnam Veterans Memorial, which was dedicated May 21, 1983. The memorial was a joint effort with many veterans organizations and their auxiliaries, as well as businesses and individuals involved. David W. McNulty, of the Wyoming Veterans Civic Council, served as chairman of the fundraising committee. The state of Wyoming and the Veterans Administration also helped to make the memorial possible. It consists of a tall brick monument, with brass and leather engravings, surrounded by a circular area of benches and shrubbery.

Cheyenne, Wyoming: Wyoming Vietnam Veterans Memorial.

Powell, Wyoming: The stone and bronze Vietnam Memorial in Powell is flanked by Wyoming and American flags.

Powell

Donations, fundraisers, and a great deal of free labor made possible the Vietnam memorial in Powell, Wyoming. The project was started by the local V.F.W. Post 54. The city of Powell provided the site, the Wyoming and American flags, and the electricity to permanently light the marker.

The monument is built of stone and has a bronze plaque engraved with the names of six area soldiers who died in the war. It is located in front of the Chamber of Commerce office and was dedicated on Memorial Day in 1984.

Other Wyoming Memorials

Cody: Proposed state monument designed along the style of the National Vietnam Veterans Memorial in Washington, D.C.

Epilogue

Thank you, America, for all you've done to remember your Vietnam veterans.

Clark Air Force Base, Philippines: The Peace Garden.

Appendix: American Memorials in Other Countries

Germany

A single, proud American oak tree grows straight and tall at Ramstein Air Force Base in Germany beside a large rock with plaques from the National League of Families and the Red River Valley Fighter Pilots Association. When the Freedom Tree was planted in June of 1977, it was adorned with yellow ribbons in remembrance of the more than 2,400 P.O.W./M.I.A.s still in Southeast Asia. A missing man formation by the F-4 aircraft of the Eighth TAC Fighter Wing flew overhead.

Japan

Misawa Air Force Base has several memorials for Vietnam veterans. They are (1) The Land Memorial Ski Lodge, Building 1482 on the base, with plaque dedicating the building to Airman First Class Charles D. Land; (2) a monument to American P.O.W./M.I.A.s, located at the base's flagpole in front of Wing Headquarters, dedicated in 1976; (3) Leftwich Park, where a monument honors TSgt. Raymond F. Leftwich (dedicated in 1983); (4) a monument honoring Airman First Class Daniel G. Reese, located near Building 1555 (dedicated in 1983); and (5) the Gosser Memorial Golf Course, dedicated in 1983 to Delbert L. Gosser (a monument is located at the clubhouse).

Philippines

Clark Air Force Base in the Philippines is the location of the lovely Peace Garden, a living tribute to the people who were killed or still remain captive in Southeast Asia. The Torri Gate at the entrance is a welcoming symbol of peace and unity. The pond and landscaping in the center of the garden are in the shape of the Hebrew letter "shin," the beginning of the Hebrew word "shalom," or peace.

Index

Page numbers in **boldface** *indicate photographs.*